DRESSAGE
The Seat, Aids and Exercises

FRONTISPIECE Anthony Crossley and Burak, in competition at Windsor, 1984

PELHAM HORSEMASTER SERIES

DRESSAGE
The Seat, Aids and Exercises

Anthony Crossley

Drawings by Patricia Frost

PELHAM BOOKS · LONDON

PELHAM BOOKS
Published by the Penguin Group
27 Wrights Lane, London W8 5TZ, England
Viking Penguin Inc., 40 West 23rd Street, New York, New York 10010, USA
Penguin Books Australia Ltd, Ringwood, Victoria, Australia
Penguin Books Canada Ltd, 2801 John Street, Markham, Ontario, Canada L3R 1B4
Penguin Books (NZ) Ltd, 182–190 Wairau Road, Auckland 10, New Zealand

Penguin Books Ltd, Registered Offices: Harmondsworth, Middlesex, England

First published 1988

Made and printed in Great Britain by
Butler & Tanner Ltd, Frome, Somerset
Phototypeset by Wilmaset, Birkenhead, Wirral

British Library Cataloguing in Publication Data
Crossley, Anthony
    Dressage: the seat, aids and exercises.
    1. Livestock: Horses. Riding. Dressage
    I. Title
    798.2'3

    ISBN 0–7207–1777–9

FRONT COVER World and European Champions Anne-Grethe Jensen and Marzog
in a display at Copenhagen, 1985.

CONTENTS

v

Preface

IN MY LAST book, DRESSAGE *An Introduction*,* I tried to provide readers with a clear picture of how the equestrian activity now known universally as dressage has developed over the last two hundred years; its aims, purposes and modern standards; and some insight into its intricacies. I hoped to make its processes and its outward appearances intelligible and thereby more enjoyable to inexperienced spectators as well as to potential practitioners. I hoped also to contribute to closing the gap between the intellectual approach to the subject of those two potentially disparate groups of people, the rider and the spectator; a coming together that is essential if dressage riding is to maintain its significance and value as a civilised and civilising activity.

This new book, DRESSAGE *The Seat, Aids and Exercises* is written as a direct sequel to its predecessor in that it moves on from understanding to doing. It attempts to provide, in simple terms, the essential details of the techniques that properly trained riders should employ while doing their work.

For the spectator, this knowledge and insight will further enhance his ability to assess the good and the bad in what he sees and will thereby deepen his interest and his understanding of the art as a whole.

For the rider, or the potential rider, a sound knowledge of those same tested and proven details of techniques will ensure that he sets out fully and efficiently equipped on his long journey in search of equestrian excellence. If he starts right and then adheres relentlessly to the straight and narrow path, determinedly resisting all temptation

*Pelham Books, 1984

1

to relax his standards in favour of seemingly easier routes, he will make steady progress without the time-wasting journeys back down the snakes before starting once more, chastened but wiser, up the ladders.

This book contains the basic rules, the standing orders, for effective and efficient communication between rider and horse. Communication is achieved by 'aids' which, to be effective, must be both precise and consistent and, to be efficient, must be economic and minimal in effort, range and visibility. The further a rider's aids deviate from those simple but basic criteria, the cruder they inevitably become and the more they flout the whole aesthetic of fine riding. And the more also they will inhibit the peace of mind, the happiness and the willing cooperation of the horse.

No one would deny that the horse's best wish must be to work with a rider who seems to be nothing more than an extension of himself. He must surely long for that perfect harmony between the two beings, no less than does the rider, that is so aptly spelt out in the International Rules for Dressage as when 'the horse gives the impression of doing of his own accord what is required of him'. That happy state would never occur if methods of communication were crude, rough, excessive or forceful. To achieve such a state of happy harmony, with all the aesthetic pleasures that accrue to himself and to the spectator, the rider must from the start train himself as well as his horse to work with and towards the highest possible degree of finesse in his methods and techniques.

An essential part of this book is the short study, to be found in the final chapter, of some of the physical exercises for both horse and rider, to be undertaken both together and, in the latter case, alone. The exercises for the horse, though not usually practised in dressage displays or competitions, play a vital part in preparation for the more formal work, and without them the ultimate achievement of that formal work will almost certainly be severely restricted.

Since no horse can be better than his rider, it is natural and logical that every serious rider must ensure that his own body is trained to be at least as fit and supple and strong and balanced as he hopes his horse will be. That desireable physical state will never be achieved merely and only by riding. Left to their own devices, a few and rare individuals may be 'not too bad', but none will be excellent unless they undertake regular exercises which they can do either in a class or in the privacy of their bedroom. Similar exercises form an integral part of training in virtually all other forms of physical activity, most famously and appropriately in schools for ballet dancers of all ages where long hours are spent daily and throughout working life 'on the bar', as opposed to the relatively short periods spent actually dancing.

Among dressage riders the world over, these preparatory and personal exercises are all too frequently skimped or even totally neglected, many riders in their arrogance believing that it is sufficient if their horses alone are forced to be loose and supple. Those riders seemingly forget that their own physical deficiencies will directly and inevitably inhibit and restrict their horse's performance through the discomfort they themselves inflict. In a ballet pas de deux, the performance of the prima donna will be ruined by any ineptitude in her partner.

For dressage riders, there are three mottoes that deserve pride of place over the door of every stable:

1 No horse can be better than his rider.
2 If the pupil has not learnt, the teacher has not taught.
3 It is always the rider's fault; never the horse's.

Introduction

THE AIDS, WHICH is the common name for the means by which a rider communicates his wishes to his horse, are made up from and share some or all of the following aspects:

1 *An intelligible message*, which functions somewhat like the pulsations that flow along a telephone wire to be readily and clearly interpreted at the receiving end, provided that the receiver has learnt the language, even if it is sent in morse-code. Such would certainly include clicking the tongue to encourage the horse to step-lively, or the vibrating leg aid to demand a trot from a walk.

2 *A degree of physio-psychological persuasion and dominance.* For example, the forward pressure of the seat bones to urge the horse forward with greater energy, or a drawn-back leg to obtain a turn-on-the-forehand.

3 *A degree of mechanical compulsion* but never amounting to force. Such would include the action of one rein to induce the horse to turn in that direction, or of both reins to induce a halt. Only the rein aids, and there are several of them, can effectively apply this direct mechanical compulsion.

In practice, almost all aids contain elements of the first two types, and none of them should be used with force. The rider should always endeavour to accentuate and rely upon the underlying psychological element.

In this study there are references to the various aids under the name of their respective source, i.e.

The aids of the loin/seat/weight, abbreviated as The Seat.

The aids of the Leg.

The aids of the Reins.

There are innumerable variations and potential combinations of aids at the disposal of a competent rider and there is an overriding need to study the ability of the horse to understand the respective languages. For that to happen, it is of prime importance that the rider should be consistent in what he does and should keep the language simple. The horse then has to be taught, and must learn, the whole alphabet of aids and must subsequently acquire the habit of responding appropriately to each and all of them for no better reason than that it will please him to cooperate and, to some extent, even to comply for the sheer physical enjoyment of doing strenuous and exciting things. But the horse must also learn from experience that there are certain not-so-pleasurable sanctions that are liable to follow his failure to comply with any reasonable request made of him.

Since, with the exception of those few unattractive and rarely used rein-aids, the horse cannot be forced to do anything against his will, it behoves the intelligent rider to make it his first task to learn to use all the aids available to him in a manner likely to induce the maximum willing cooperation from the horse. Once that process of mutual and happy cooperation has been established, through a mixture of tact, trust, and habit, it can be developed and polished as the training partnership progresses over the years until it becomes so refined that all aids from the rider become virtually invisible to the spectator; the rider seems only to have to think to obtain the required responses and actions; and the horse 'gives the impression of doing of his own accord what is required of him'.

But to achieve that very high degree of finesse at the end of the day, the same alphabet of correct, logical, simple and gentle aids must be used from the very beginning and then maintained and practised with undeviating persistence.

The rider must never give way to the temptation to say that he or his horse are 'different'; that the so-called correct aids do not seem to work in his case; that unorthodox aids must surely be justified to overcome his exceptional problems. Inexperienced riders will often be prey to such misgivings in moments of difficulty or when some new problem confronts them. But nothing is exceptional; nothing is unprecedented; and the temptations must be rejected ruthlessly and as a matter of discipline. To give way to them is to turn down the slippery slope that will always end in ugly riding habits, an unaesthetic performance, and a more or less confused and inadequately trained horse.

There is only one way to ride for those who accept that dressage riding is potentially an art, or at least a skill with an appreciable artistic element, and that is the classical way; the way that has been developed over the last four hundred years by riders of many countries who have spent their entire lives in the study of the subject and who are now written into history as the Masters; the way that is today accepted virtually without argument by all the great schools of equitation dedicated to the tradition of fine horsemanship, whether in Austria, Sweden, Germany, France, Portugal, Spain, Switzerland, Russia or elsewhere.

Britain, since the end of the seventeenth century, has lacked such a school and has only recently, in the last forty years, begun to search for the academic information that must be the foundation for our renaissance. Without a national centre for such studies; without national even if itinerant professors, the search will be long and hard and will have largely to be undertaken by each individual who professes an interest either as trainer or amateur.

There are few subjects in this world that can be studied in detail without the use of books that carry forward the findings and teachings of the old or recent masters, and dressage riding is certainly no exception. This book claims to provide guidance for students, its contents being based solely on information derived from the received wisdom of the great riders of the past.

Before starting on the studies contained in the following chapters, we should remind ourselves, and thereafter remember, that although the many forms of Aid will mainly be discussed singly in their own right, in practice it is a golden and all-pervading rule of good riding that no one aid should ever be used in isolation by itself. Every message sent to the horse should be a combination of all the aid-media; the media of the back/seat/weight, the media of the legs, and the media of the hands or reins. Any one of these forms, if used in isolation, will at best be ineffective and more often harmful. Equally important is the principle that the sequence of pattern of their employment is invariably the same:

1 The correct, balanced rider-position together with a forward bracing of the loin; the prerequisites for any refined aid.

2 The leg aids that activate the horse; that create or maintain impulsion; that must always precede any rein-aid.

3 The hands and reins that restrain or direct the action.

4 Again the rider's loin/seat/weight, the central combination that coordinates and modulates all the other aids and their effects.

Readers will find that in certain cases the actual movements for which appropriate aids are described will themselves be described in some detail under a sub-heading introduction. These introductions have been inserted to cover the vital and obvious importance of the student knowing precisely what he intends to achieve, and precisely what reaction he expects from his horse, before he begins the process of doing it. If he lacks that clear knowledge and understanding, his aids like his mind will be muddled. And so will his horse.

Throughout the book, all descriptions of equine movement are based on the now-current knowledge, derived from modern veterinary research, that the horse's spine is incapable, for all practical purposes, of any lateral flexibility between the point where the rider sits and the tail.

CHAPTER ONE

The Seat: Rider Position

Part 1 THE THEORY OF THE SEAT AS AN AID

IT IS IMPOSSIBLE to talk seriously about the aids except on the assumption that the rider is sitting correctly on his horse and can maintain that position at all paces and as long as he is in the saddle. That position, or manner of sitting in the saddle, is the first and foremost matter to which every aspiring dressage rider must give his attention. Everything he does throughout his riding life will be significantly marred if he does not put himself right in this respect in the first place.

We need not be thinking in terms of pedantic or exact perfection, but only of the broad principles of what is correct, based on quite simple rules of physical mechanics. These rules are widely known and established, and they have to be understood, adopted and rigorously followed. That adoption should not cause any serious problem to any person of normal physique and intellect, provided only that he genuinely understands what he is required to do and the reasons for it. But the sad fact is that, in so many cases, no adequate explanations are given by the riding teacher to the rider who has not taken the trouble, with the help of a little reading, to work it out for himself. In such cases the rider starts in a fog and remains in it. It is only later on that such a rider begins to discover the difficulties created by his largely self-inflicted shortcomings, and by that time all kinds of bad habits of mind and muscle have become more or less embedded and are quite difficult to eradicate. Passing years do not make the eradication any easier.

There is of course no excuse for a riding teacher who does not bother to teach, unless it be that he has not himself been properly trained to do so. And in that case he is not qualified for his job. No self-respecting drill-sergeant has any great difficulty in instilling, within a few weeks, the habit of good posture into a large squad of raw and awkward recruits. There are many similarities between the problems of the drill sergeant and the riding teacher, and, to make it easier for the latter, he seldom has to deal with more than half-a-dozen pupils at once, and quite frequently only one.

The claim of Rider Position to a chapter of its own in this book about aids is founded on two hypotheses of almost equal importance:

1 No aid of seat, weight, leg or hand can be applied correctly, and therefore efficiently and consistently, unless the basic position of the rider is correct. The two aspects are tightly interrelated. And more than anything else this refers to the rider's body from the seat bones to the top of his head. All the aids have their origin in that arsenal; and if its own status is flawed or weak, the aids will themselves be flawed or weak with the inevitable result that the rider will be operating at a disadvantage. But since dressage riding is known to be a very difficult craft to master, it cannot be sensible to start off with anything but the best possible tools and aids.

2 The manner in which a rider sits on, or in, the saddle constitutes, whether he likes it or not, an aid in itself. It cannot help but influence the horse for better or for worse; to his advantage or to his disadvantage; to make his work easier or more difficult; so it had better be good. It will say things in a language that should at least complement and not contradict the language used to convey more deliberate and intentional signals and requests.

It follows that if the unintentional influence of the seat-position contradicts or appears to be at cross-purposes with the intentional aids of the rider, be they weight, seat, leg or hand aids, there will be confusion; the horse will be unable to understand what is wanted; he will cease to pay attention; and he will become sour.

On the other hand, if the seat-position is correct according to the classic laws of equestrian mechanics, it will not only form the perfect base and source of all the intentional aids; it will at the same time and of its own accord enable and encourage the horse to move freely and unconstrainedly which, it need hardly be said, is the ultimate purpose of all the other more deliberate aids. It will begin quietly, and help to maintain, the various processes that can then be developed in ever increasing intricacy by the intentional and conventional aids.

Part 2 THE SEAT AT THE HALT

Before we study these two complementary aspects of the rider–position in detail, i.e. the seat in its own right and the intentional aids, we must first check that we know precisely what that position amounts to at the halt or, as it were, on the drawing board. The activity aspects, when the horse is in motion, will then be more readily intelligible.

We need a seat that will permit the rider to sit in the saddle for long periods in perfect balance, without muscular effort, and totally relaxed. To take those three basic requirements separately:

1 We need the perfect balance so that we do not have to struggle to retain it, or even to avoid falling off, by gripping with the legs which would impede the use of our limbs for giving signals and instructions; and so that our own imbalance will not create imbalance in the horse, which it assuredly would.

2 We need the habit of being able to hold that balanced position unimpaired for long periods so that we can ride our horse to the very best of our ability for as long as may be necessary, and not just for occasional short periods of crisis or peak requirement. Balance alone can provide the ability to sit for those longer periods without effort. If we lack that balance we shall have to begin to work and to get tired; we shall always then be a little behind instead of with the movement of the horse.

3 We need to be totally relaxed from top to toe, in body and in mind, so that we can remain fully sensitive, fully alert, and free from the inevitably paralysing effect of muscular tension. Without that relaxation we can never hope to achieve the state of being at one with our horse that is both the aim and the achievement of every good horseman. Again, balance is the essential prerequisite of relaxation. Without balance, relaxation is impossible.

Knitting all these things together, and because of the non-practical or abstract quality of dressage, we need to look as elegant as we possibly can. Tension destroys elegance; elegance means poise; poise means balance; and balance helps the horse.

As we develop this study, the overriding importance of the relaxed and balanced seat will become more and more evident. If the seat is true in those respects, all the other aids become, almost unconsciously but progressively, merely an extension of the seat. It is, as we have already said, the source and the beginning of all the aids, and will do most of the work for us in the easiest possible way.

The Seat in Detail (at the halt)

The moment the rider lowers himself into the saddle he should adopt the posture that will remain unchanged to any significant degree until the time comes to dismount. If only for the sake of his horse he should never, for any reason whatsoever, allow himself to 'slop about' or adopt strange attitudes. Such negligence can easily become the seeds of bad habits. It should be regarded as an honour and a duty to sit perfectly at all times. Any failures or change must inevitably result in some degree of discomfort, and therefore fatigue, for the horse.

However, the adoption of the correct posture does not initially occur naturally and without conscious effort, at any rate for the beginner. The rider will need to think quite deliberately about a few matters each time he mounts until such time as the habit has been established so that eventually the seat 'finds itself' unconsciously.

Whereas the various actions or checks will in practice happen almost simultaneously, they can be written down and memorised in logical sequence. It is a sequence that will be repeated many, many times during active riding and will not be fully effective if it is in any way reversed.

First, the seat bones are lowered into the lowest part of the saddle or, if that point is not clear, as far forward as is comfortable. They should then be balanced, if the saddle has been well designed, over the centre of gravity of the horse, thus causing the minimum adverse effect on the latter and being subject to the minimum disturbance to itself from the horse's movement, as if it were poised over the centre point of a see-saw.

Second, immediately the seat bones touch the saddle, the top of the pelvis, or *hipbones,* must be gently but firmly rocked forward so as to bring them into the same vertical alignment as the seat bones and the shoulders. Left to themselves, as with any untutored athlete or

11

FIG 1 **A good position.** Note alignment of pelvis and concavity of the loin; the height of the hands; the verticality of the head and torso.

gymnast, they will tend to collapse backwards behind that line, as when sitting in a lounging type of chair. But by bringing them forward as described, the whole torso comes into balance.

The action of the pelvis that the rider has just taken is exactly the same as that adopted by any child who has been told to 'sit up properly' at table, and the resulting position is exactly the same as that used by most 'respectable' people in polite society in the nineteenth century, before the invention of lounging chairs.

It will be noticed that the tipping-forward of the top of the pelvis has resulted in a slightly concave line of the spine in the lumbar area. This is perfectly correct and is indeed an essential feature of a good seat, and it must not be confused with the abhorred hollow-back which has to do with not sitting fully and effectively on the seat bones but rather on the thigh or crotch. If the rider checks and frequently rechecks that his weight is truly on his seat bones, he need have no fear of developing a hollow-back, providing only that his lower spine remains supple and unconstrained.

Third, the head and neck must be brought back, if they are not already there, into the same alignment as the seat-hip-shoulders. The neck is so flexible that it will not of necessity conform to the position of the rest of the torso and it must therefore be given special attention. But it will have been noticed that the forward positioning of the pelvis, as already described, has of itself a tendency to erect the shoulders and the neck, so that the completion of the overall line will not be difficult. On the other hand the head, since it is fixed largely in front of the neck vertebrae, will itself have a tendency to fall forward and to carry the neck with it; so a degree of mind-over-matter is necessary to counter this problem.

The carriage of the head and neck is nevertheless of very great importance since the head is heavy, weighing perhaps between eight and ten pounds, and will inevitably, if out of balance, cause a significant disturbance to the balance not only of the rider but of the horse as well. The latter point may not sound very worrying to a beginner who is concerned only with relatively simple forms of training, but it can mean the difference between success and failure when it comes later on to movements that require the horse to remain in perfect balance for relatively prolonged periods to perform such movements as sequence flying-changes. Under those circumstances, unless the rider has thoroughly established the correct habit, it is likely to fail him at the crucial moments when he has many other things on his mind.

Fourth, the legs, from the hip joint to the heel, must be quite consciously allowed to hang down by their own weight into their natural position as directed purely by gravity and the shape of the horse. The latter, combined with the muscles of the human thigh, will suffice to ensure that they do not naturally fall into one vertical line; and there must be no forced stretching or gripping with those thigh muscles or with any other part of the leg.

The knee will always be somewhat bent and the ankle, without being forced, should be more closed than open.

It is often advisable, immediately after mounting, or even during an active ride, to lift the whole leg away from its contact with the horse to check that the muscles really are relaxed, and in particular that the big muscles at the back of the upper thigh are not interfering with the contact between the flat inner thigh and the saddle.

Fifth, the toes, or the foot as a whole, should not be encouraged to drop towards the ground as to do so involves a somewhat unnatural and forced stretching tension of the ankle, calf and upper thigh muscles. In any case, as we shall see later, there are good reasons why the toes should always remain higher than the heels when riding normally with stirrups. Stretching the feet down, or allowing them to collapse, should be restricted to the occasional and short-term exercise to loosen the ankle joint if it seems to have become stiff.

Sixth, if the *heel* is allowed to hang quite naturally and by gravity as prescribed, it will be found that the legs will of their own accord fall into a position in which the lower leg will be sloping slightly behind the vertical with the heel more or less in the same vertical line as the head, shoulders and seat bones. Thus the entire body, with the exception of the forearms, will be reacting to the same gravity-line, and no muscular effort will be needed to keep them that way. However, we should not be too pedantic about the heel being exactly under the seat bones. Slight differences in the shape of horse, rider or saddle can make that criterion difficult to achieve with precision, and in any case the legs are always subject to slight movement when applying the different leg-aids. It is, on the whole, more important that the lower leg should be lying as close as possible to the rear edge of the girth; that the heel should sink below the toes; and that the stirrup leather should hang vertically.

With those three criteria achieved, there will be no need for muscular contraction to hold the leg in any other or more awkward place. The verticality of the stirrup-leather is a great tell-tale. Left to itself it will, through gravity, always be vertical. It stands to reason that, if it is not vertical, either forward or rearward, it must be being held so by muscular action from the rider's legs. If that is happening, the legs cannot be relaxed and the rider is breaking one of the prime rules.

All weight should now flow down through one line of gravity into the heel where it can be gently absorbed, so far as the weight of the legs is concerned, by the downward feathering of the ankle joint just behind the stirrup. That downward flow, which is primarily responsible for giving the rider the so-called deep seat, will not occur if it is blocked by any clamping of the legs onto the horse, by fixing the knee, by stiffening the ankle, or by pressing down onto the toes. It is worth repeating once again that the whole leg below the hipjoint, unless specifically moved for some temporary leg aid, must remain at all times hanging down by its own weight.

The lower part of the leg, encased in its boot, does not naturally hang quite vertically. The weight of the foot that protrudes only in front of the leg will cause the leg itself, from the knee downwards, to hang, if left to its own devices, at a slight angle behind the vertical, thus laying it diagonally across the girth, with the knee a little in front and the heel a little behind. Any subsequent action of the calf-muscles will then operate on the back edge of, or immediately behind, the girth; in other words 'on the girth' or 'at the girth'. That is the area where the horse is most sensitive and also most flexible in his body, and can therefore most readily respond to the rider's messages through the leg, as we shall see later. But meantime, and as from the first moment of sitting in the saddle, the leg will be lying in light contact with the horse in the best possible place from which messages can be passed without the need for any visible or disturbing movements.

Seventh, with the foundation of the body and legs established, the reins are picked up with *the hands* coming immediately into a direct line between the rider's elbows and the bit, when viewed from the side. The retention of this straight line is of inestimable importance in its effect on the sensitivity of the contact with the bit. It is not always easy for the rider himself to check this point accurately, but he can quite easily use the rule-of-thumb that, under all normal circumstances, his hands should and will be a handsbreadth clear of and above the wither. They will then carry themselves and will never rely, or even appear to rely on contact with the withers.

The back of the hands, facing outwards, should be in a straight line with the outer part of the forearm, or perhaps turned fractionally inwards; never outwards. The thumbs should always be uppermost and the fingers lightly closed.

The length of the rein should initially be such that the upper arm will hang naturally and vertically down with the elbow lightly brushing the waist and fractionally in front of the hips. Only when the upper arm is more or less vertical can it hold its position without muscular effort. Relaxation = no muscular tension = sensitivity.

The knuckles of the two hands should not touch; should never be more than two or three inches apart, depending on the movement being executed; and neither should ever be allowed to cross the line of the horse's neck.

It is vital that the hands, permanently in contact by means of the reins with the horse's extremely sensitive mouth, should themselves be as light and as sensitive as they possibly can be. The position and method of holding the hands just described is the only one that fulfills that requirement. All other positions such as having the backs of the hands uppermost, or bending the wrists outwards, or overbending them inwards, inevitably make for stiffness and loss of sensitivity in the feeling of the hands on the reins.

We have outlined the correct and best position for the hands, but it must not be thought that they are fixed, rigid or immovable. They should be still in relation to the horse's mouth, but the horse as he moves is not fixed into any permanent mould and there will be room for slight if nigh invisible movements of the hands to compensate, and to encourage and to make requests. The hands of the good rider will always be alive and will move, but no one will notice and the horse will not be disturbed.

Seat Summary

The seat we have been describing has been given many names by different authorities, all of them valid and none of them contradictory. The balanced seat is probably the most popular and regularly used, but it is also classical, efficient and elegant. It might also, and not unreasonably, be called the easy seat in that it makes working-life easy for both horse and rider, saving effort and inducing calmness. It is totally natural in essence, for the job in hand.

In order to ensure a thorough grasp of all that is involved and required in the classical seat, we have studied, in considerable detail and in its separate parts, just how the rider should settle himself into the saddle. But since the detailed study is probably too long for most people to memorise, it will be as well to summarise its salient points, and that can hardly be done better than by quoting from the relevant passage in the F.E.I. Rules for Dressage (article 417) which says:

'All the movements should be obtained without apparent effort of the rider. He should be well balanced, with his loins and hips supple, thighs and legs steady and well stretched downwards. The upper part of the body easy, free and erect, with the hands low and close together without however touching each other or the horse and with the thumbs at the highest point; the elbows and arms close to the body, enabling the rider to follow the movements of the horse smoothly and freely and to apply his aids imperceptibly. *This is the only position making it possible for the rider to school his horse progressively and correctly.'*

Those concise phrases generalise wisely, since guidance in the form of guidelines rather than rigid rules are appropriate for living beings, although they may be insufficient for most beginners without the back-up of the detailed and explanatory references to what is required from each and every part of the body. But the two aspects, the general and the detailed, hang together, and anyone who violates either will be doing so at his peril and to the certain detriment of his horsemanship.

Part 3 THE SEAT IN ACTION

The Passive Seat

Having followed and understood the detail and the guidelines for sitting correctly, efficiently and elegantly in the saddle at the halt, the rider must face the somewhat more difficult task of retaining that position in all its detail, or at least with hardly perceptible variations, when the horse is in motion, in walk, trot and canter. If he is really sitting correctly at the halt; and if he has been properly briefed by his instructor, or by his reading and studies, about the mechanical functions of the correct seat, he will find that any difficulties that he encounters on the move can be relatively easily and quickly overcome. Indeed, the details of the correct seat have been specifically designed to that end.

There is however just one overriding requirement which is that the rider must discipline himself to remain relaxed in all his muscles; not tensed-up; breathing freely; and mentally calm. To achieve that mental and physical state of relaxation he must make progress slowly at first, tackling each new experience one at a time and little by little until he has gained the necessary confidence in himself.

Every gymnast or trick-cyclist will confirm that relaxation is the first essential for balance, and balance is the essence of horsemanship if only for the benefit of the horse. But relaxation must not, repeat not, result in any alteration to the overall posture of the rider which must always, under all circumstances, comply with those clearly expressed F.E.I. guidelines.

The crux of the problems connected with retaining a true seat when the horse is in motion lies in the fact that horses do not move smoothly along the ground like a bicycle. They progress, in the walk, in a series of not-uncomfortable heaves which do not cause any significant inconvenience to the rider; in the trot, in a series of small hops in quick succession, each of which definitely produces a significant disturbance and perhaps even discomfort to the uneducated or incompetent rider to the extent that his seat may effectively be rendered non-existent with a potentially damaging effect on his own and his horse's back-muscles; and in the canter, in a series of much slower leaps, beginning with a rolling-forward movement over all four legs followed by a 'take-off' in which all four legs are simultaneously off the ground, the effect of which is easier to cope with than the trot action but which is nevertheless more or less unseating to the untrained rider.

Anyone who has ever thrown a ball into the air will know how easy it is to make the ball relinquish its contact with the hand and go higher than the hand did. Any weighted body thrown up by another larger or heavier body will be subjected to the same mechanical principle and tendency. The horse throws the rider up. But flying into the air, or bumping in the saddle, is a very inefficient and uncomfortable way of riding a horse, and so ways have to be found to compensate for, or obviate, the bump so that the rider's seat bones can remain, as it were, glued to the saddle under all conditions of motion. Then he can ride without anxiety, discomfort or fatigue. Then he can feel and communicate with his horse without disturbing it. Then he is as-one with his horse. Then both parties can be happy.

The means of avoiding the tendency to bump that is a natural corollary to riding a horse in trot or canter are readily available to every rider who sits in the manner described in Part 2 of this chapter, and the key to that solution lies, above all else, in the correct positioning of the pelvis.

The top of the pelvis, it will be remembered, should be rocked forward over the seat bones so that the hips (top of the pelvis) come into the same vertical line as the shoulders and the seat bones and create a slight concavity in the region of the lumbar spine. That concavity has a vital part to play, but before explaining that part in detail, we will look for a moment at the analogy of a diving-board.

If a straight broomstick is placed vertically on a diving-board and the board is activated, the broomstick will assuredly bounce and leave its seating on the board in an increasingly irregular manner; irregular because it will not of itself retain the same rhythm as the board.

But if a piece of rope is held up so that its lower end rests on the board, there will be no displacement when the board is activated. So all the rider has to do is to ensure that he operates like the rope and not like the broomstick. It is as simple at that.

The slight concavity in the lumbar area of the rider's back that arises, as we have said, from rocking forward the pelvis, corresponds exactly to the forward curve of the rider's spine in the same area; an area where the spine is naturally very supple. The curve of the lower spine can then function exactly like the lower end of the rope on the diving-board. The rope bulges or ripples more as the board rises higher, but the hand holding the upper end does not have to move. Similarly, the spine will curve forward in a more pronounced manner as the horse and saddle rise under the rider with each hop or leap, thus absorbing the upward thrust within the area of the pelvis and without causing any disturbance to the upper part of the torso or the head. The lower spine is thus acting as an efficient shock-absorber to nullify the upward thrusts of the horse and to permit the rider to sit firmly, quietly and consistently in the saddle.

There is one further problem which does not arise with the diving-board. With every hop or leap, the horse is moving forward as well as upward. If the rider does not do something to compensate for that factor, he will always be tending to be left behind; to slip towards or over the back of the saddle. To make that compensation he has only, by bracing forward the muscles of his loin with each jump of the horse, to ensure that his pelvis keeps rocking forward a little so that he will always be 'going along with' the movement, an action that is sometimes though less appropriately referred to as 'following' the movement. The rider need not concern himself much with the rocking motion because that will happen of its own accord as the result of the constant pressing forward of the hips. The latter point is where his attention should lie, and it will have the additional and beneficial effect of straightening the shoulders and raising or erecting the neck since it is virtually impossible, as was found by the child when told to 'sit up' at table, to position the pelvis correctly and collapse the shoulders at the same time.

The vital process of 'going along with the horse', mainly created by the bracing and pushing forward of the loins and the consequent pelvic rock, will be automatically assisted by the fact that the weight of the upper torso, each time it comes down into the saddle at the crucial moment of potential bump, will fall in a non-vertical or forward-and-downward direction towards the knees, and this will have the double effect of carrying the rider forward as well as pressing him deeper and more firmly into the saddle . . . provided the knees are not locked.

This action of the pelvis and its several and interrelated effects will occur, and must be encouraged and made use of, at all paces. It will be powerful and need careful control in trot and canter. It will be reduced to the minimum in the walk which has no jump or lift in it, though the pelvic action, also reduced to the minimum, should be maintained just as regularly in order to 'go along' with the forward thrust of the gait.

It often happens in the walk that, due to the relatively slow speed of progress, the rider will tend to lean forward, the weight of his torso then falling in front of his seat bones, and therefore nullifying their driving influence. To ensure against this happening, the rider should remind himself that 'the pelvis must always lead the torso', and never the other way round.

We can now begin to see that once the horse has been put into motion, especially in trot and canter, the basic mechanism of the horse/rider harmony will start up of its own accord. If the rider has set the engine mechanism efficiently, with all the components correctly positioned and balanced in relation to all the others, it will function smoothly and efficiently and with little effort from the rider himself. It will not necessarily be working under 'full throttle', at maximum efficiency, but it will be alive and ready for more throttle. The key to success lies in the integrated operation of:

1 The forward thrusting of the loin, or rocking pelvis, and with it,
2 The forward and shock-absorbing flexions of the lower or lumbar spine.

In the simplest terms, the horse will make a series of upward and forward thrusts, according to the selected gait; the rider, being lighter than the horse, will be thrown upward with a tendency, but only a tendency, to leave the saddle; the rider will not leave the saddle because of the shock-absorbing action of the forward-flexing lumbar spine; the horse begins to subside to the ground, allowing room for the more or less fully flexed lumbar spine to reflex back to its more normal posture, but not so far as to allow the hips to fall behind the vertical shoulder-line, and therefore still retaining some degree of forward flexion; the spine remains ready in position to absorb the next upward thrust that will occur with the next step or stride.

The horse does the work and provides the energy; the rider's own weight and spring-like lumbar spine do the rest . . . provided only that the pelvis, and with it the spine, are kept forward in their right place in the overall structure by the constant and essential bracing of the back.

And that is all that is needed for sitting efficiently, though more or less passively, on a horse in action. In effect that vital though sometimes invisible pelvic action is the key to good riding. It constantly corrects the rider's posture, especially that of the upper torso. It carries the rider along with the movement. And it keeps the rider's weight flowing deep into the saddle. It minimises the inconvenience to the horse caused by the very existence of the rider on his back, and it encourages the horse to carry his rider forward. It is thus acting as an aid to free forward movement.

The Influential Seat

We have talked so far only about the means by which the rider learns to sit still and in perfect balance at the halt and in all the gaits, to his own and his horse's maximum convenience and comfort but without making any great demands on either partner. But practical horsemanship requires that the rider should be able to make many and various demands on his horse's skill and energy; demands that are both positive, precise, consistent and humane. Such demands are made by means of signals or aids and, as we already know, those signals all have their roots and origins in the rider's seat. Every aid from leg or hand needs an initiating and supporting function from the seat, a function that is provided by the very simple expedient of increasing the power of the muscle bracing action, that action that we have already noted as necessary to push the hipbones forward under the torso. The effect of this increased tension in the loin muscles will be:

1 To reduce, but not nullify, the forward flexibility of the lumbar spine, thereby giving the shock absorber a shorter, stronger and more powerful action.

2 To increase the influence of the seat bones on the saddle and therefore on the horse's back muscles.

3 To cause the spring-like shape of the lower spine, still acting in a forward and downward manner, to draw forward the seat bones on the saddle, thus exerting a distinct forward-urging influence on the horse. The seat bones will be acting in the same way as does the top of one's thumb when pressed forward (towards the knuckles) on the back of the other hand. Without moving on the skin (though the skin will wrinkle), it will exert a definite urge for the whole hand to move forward, the concave back of the thumb retaining its concavity. This demonstrates precisely the forward-urging action of the loin-activated seat bones on the horse's back.

There is nothing else that the seat can do in that respect. It can in this way help to maintain, if only psychologically, but it cannot create, the forward impulsion that in fact only the legs can actually generate. We shall be referring to the latter point again, later on.

Summary of the Seat

We have made a fairly comprehensive study of the basic aspects of the classical seat and its importance in classical riding in its basic forms. Its acquisition is an absolute necessity for the rider who hopes to ride with maximum comfort and to develop maximum skills and pleasure from the horse. During the process of this study we have seen that the adoption of classical or correct posture by the rider results in the payment of three very big dividends:

1 It sets up the mechanism that will ensure that the balance of the rider and therefore of the horse will not be disturbed.

2 It forms a sound foundation for all controlled and controlling aids.

3 It enables the rider to remain relaxed and supple which in turn allows the mechanism to operate automatically as a gentle aid for free,

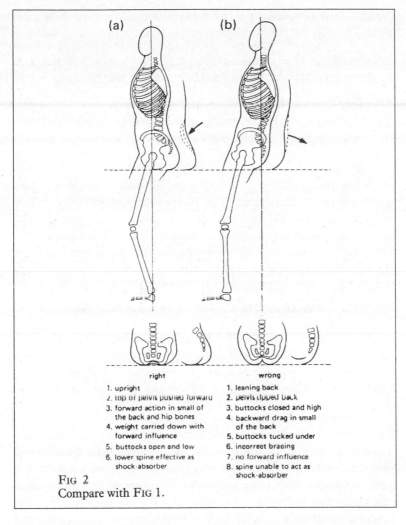

(a)   (b)

right   wrong

1. upright
2. top of pelvis pushed forward
3. forward action in small of
   the back and hip bones
4. weight carried down with
   forward influence
5. buttocks open and low
6. lower spine effective as
   shock-absorber

1. leaning back
2. pelvis tipped back
3. buttocks closed and high
4. backward drag in small
   of the back
5. buttocks tucked under
6. incorrect bracing
7. no forward influence
8. spine unable to act as
   shock-absorber

FIG 2
Compare with FIG 1.

forward movement. Any further increase in the power and influence
of that aid is then achieved by merely bracing more strongly the
muscles of the loin, or small of the back, without in any way altering
the basic operation of the mechanism.

In short, it makes riding relatively easy and also helps the horse.
The fact that it also and throughout the process assists the rider to
look elegant and effortless is a final bonus.

23

Some Common Faults of the Seat

(1) *Sitting with the seat bones too far back in the saddle*, behind its lowest point. This is a serious fault which has several bad effects. It is often referred to as a Chair Seat, because the rider sits as he would in a chair, not over his feet.

a The rider's weight falls behind the horse's centre of gravity and, even more importantly, nearer to the weakest point of the horse's back where it is least able to support it, in the area of the loins or lumbar vertebrae.

b With the rider sitting in that position it immediately becomes more difficult, or even impossible, for the horse's back to swing with the impulsion from the quarters or for the quarters to engage. The rider, in effect, flattens his horse's back.

c Assuming that the rider's legs remain more or less in their normal and correct position on the girth, and with the stirrup leathers hanging vertically, the rider will clearly not be in balance within himself and through one vertical line of gravity. There will be one line through the shoulders and seat bones to the ground, and another through his knees and lower legs to the ground. He will not be balanced over his feet and will be breaking the golden rule that, if the horse were to be suddenly removed, the rider would land happily and perfectly balanced on both feet on the ground. If he can pass that test, he can claim to have been in perfect balance while his horse was under him.

(2) *Holding the lower leg too far forward.* Remember that it would not be too far forward, that is to say with the stirrup leather in front of the vertical, if it was truly being 'allowed to hang down' of its own accord (see early part of this chapter). For the effect of gravity to have been overcome, it must have been pushed there and held there by direct muscular action, which in itself is wrong. The cure lies in releasing the muscular tension that is holding it in the forward position so that the leg will immediately fall back to its normal, natural and correct position which, due to the weight of the foot, is slightly behind the vertical, but with the stirrup-leather actually vertical.

To summarise the ill effects of this fault, apart from the muscular tension involved, it constantly tends to push the seat back in the

24

Fig 2A

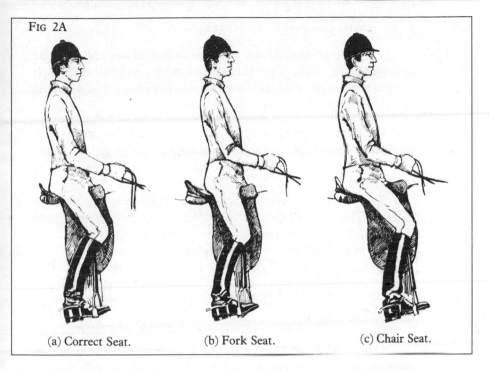

| (a) Correct Seat. | (b) Fork Seat. | (c) Chair Seat. |

saddle; it breaks the balance line of the rider who would not 'land on his feet'; and it makes the leg insensitive, partly because of the muscular tension and partly because it will be lying along or over the girth instead of softly on the horseflesh immediately behind the girth where the horse is most sensitive.

(3) *Holding the lower leg too far back* Here again remember that it would not be in that position if was truly 'hanging naturally' and relaxed. Again, the check is whether the stirrup leather is, or is not, being allowed to hang vertically.

The ill effects of this fault are similar to those connected with the leg being too far forward:

a The leg must be under a degree of permanent muscular tension in order to maintain the position. If it were not, then gravity alone would ensure its return to the normal position on the girth.

b In this false position the leg will not be in contact with the most sensitive area of the horse's body.

25

FIG 3 **Lower leg too far forward**; not hanging naturally by own weight; leather in front of the vertical.

c The heel will tend to rise and the rider will tend to press down with his toes to prevent the stirrup falling off his boot.

d The flow of the rider's weight will not be going into the heel as it should to maintain a deep and balanced seat. The rider will be sitting 'shallow' instead of deep.

e As the result of **d** above, the rider's leg will not be lengthened, as it should be, by every bracing of the back, and so every leg-aid will be to that extent weakened; the rider cannot be functioning at his best.

The cure for all these evils is simply to allow the leg to hang down naturally, by its own weight, thus obviating the need to use any muscles to hold it anywhere.

(4) *Leaning forward* If the rider leans forward in front of the vertical he has taken some of his weight off his seat bones and cannot

FIG 4 **Lower leg too far back**; not hanging naturally by own weight; leather behind the vertical.

therefore be properly in balance; he will be 'in front of the movement', and consequently not fully in control of his horse, particularly in any form of downward transition. His seat will be severely weakened. It should always feel and appear, if only for psychological reasons, as if the horse is doing his work in front of the rider's seat, not vice versa. If the torso is leading the pelvis, the rider cannot use his seat to exert a forward influence.

The cure lies in experimenting with the position of the upper body to discover the point from which the maximum weight is felt on the seat bones. Then, and only then, the body will be vertical and balanced.

(5) *Leaning back* If the rider leans back behind the vertical he will be causing all sorts of problems. The weight of his torso, affected as it must be by gravity, will act behind the vertical line through the

FIG 5 **Rider leaning forward**; in front of his horse; weight not fully on seat bones; seat not effective.

seat bones, tending instead to fall to some point nearer to the weaker parts of the horse's back. The horse will tend to flatten and the back muscles will cease to swing; with the gravity line lost, the weight will not be flowing into the heel and the seat will be weakened; because of the loss of natural balance there will inevitably be an increase in tension in the rider's back muscles which will never be properly relaxed.

The rider will be out of balance when the horse is stationary; when the horse is moving forward, he will be quite unable to 'go along' with the movement; he will be behind the movement and will have to resort to a degree of gripping with his legs to avoid gradually slipping off the back of the saddle.

So much trouble is caused by leaning back behind the vertical, but fortunately the cure is once again quite simple. Just find the position of the torso from which the maximum weight can be felt on the

FIG 6 **Rider leaning back behind the vertical**; weight of torso falls behind own centre of gravity; rider not in balance and behind, instead of with any movement.

seat bones without any support from the buttocks and without any muscle tension in the back or loin. When the horse is moving forward that position can quite easily be maintained by regularly bracing the loin muscles to move the pelvis forward and 'along with' the movement.

(6) *Lower leg not in contact with the horse* The only excusable instance of this fault is when a very long-legged rider is on a very small horse, in which case the rider has little option but to rely on his seat-aids to a greater extent than he would normally do. In all other cases the fault will arise as the result of gripping with the knees and/or tensing the muscles of the thigh and lower leg instead of allowing the whole leg to hang down naturally of its own accord.

The main weaknesses arising from this fault are:

FIG 7
(A) Lower leg not in contact (rear view)
(B), (C) and (D) Lower leg in contact (rear, side and front views). Hip bones forward to position the pelvis under the torso; head carried above the shoulders; hands in a straight line between elbow and bit with thumbs uppermost; upper arms and legs hanging naturally; toes to the front.

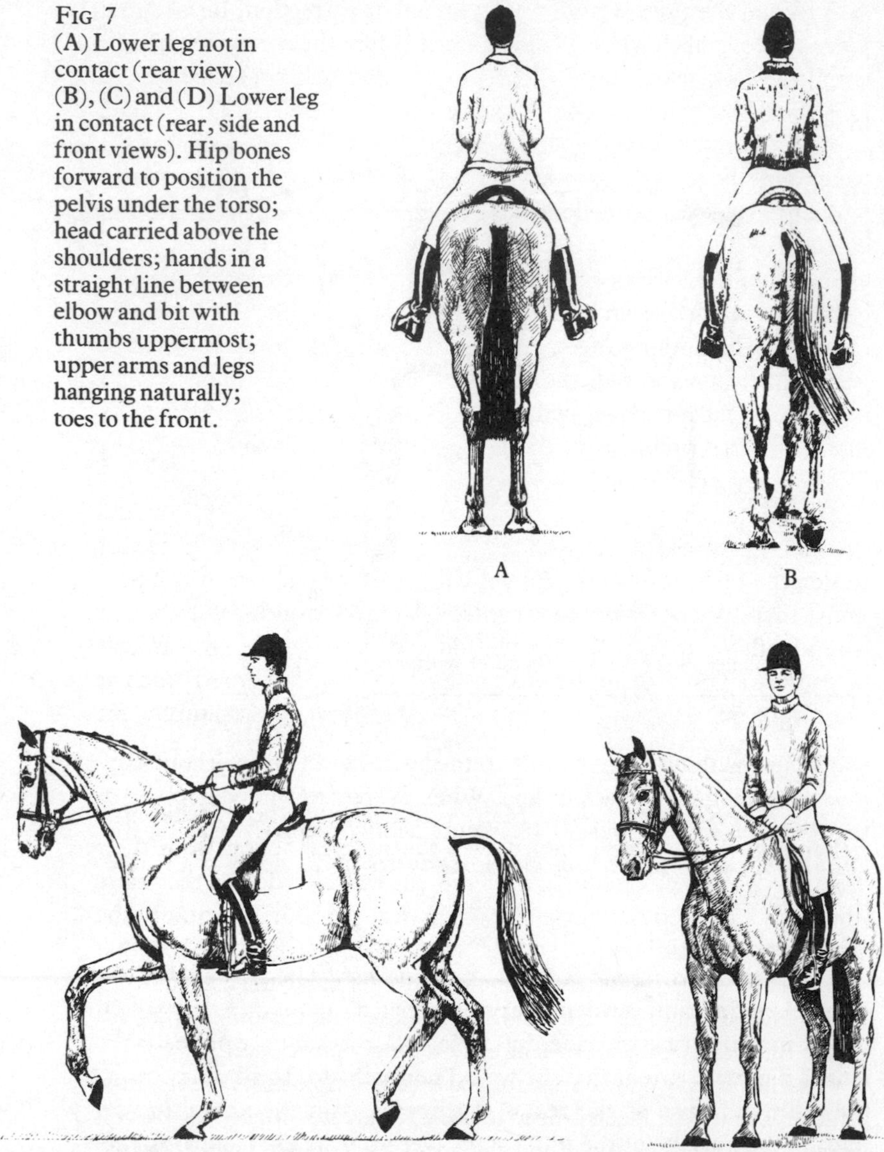

A

B

C

D

a The lower legs are one of the rider's main 'feelers', and if they are not in contact he will not be able to feel effectively what is going on.

b When the rider wishes to give an aid or correction, he will first have to move his lower legs into contact before the correction can be applied. That takes time, and the correction will consequently be mistimed and will not achieve maximum effectiveness.

c In an effort to overcome the tendency to be late with his aids the rider will be forced to use rougher, stronger or cruder aids; a tendency that will in the long run spoil the sensitive responses of his horse.

d When the legs are not in contact, there will be no communication between horse and rider and the horse will not be listening. There will be nothing to listen to. When the aid does come, it will be sudden and unexpected, the response being correspondingly jerky.

e Most but not all leg-aids should be applied intermittently and not in precise timing with the horse's stride. This ensures that the horse does not become bored and inattentive to a regular and rhythmical repetition of a leg movement. But to achieve such an aid the rider must learn to rely on the mere momentary tension of his leg inside the boot, the boot itself not being seen or felt to move. There must therefore be permanent contact, the horse waiting calmly and confidently to sense the leg-tension that will convey his rider's intentions. This rule applies just as much to those minor aids such as for 'walk on' as to the stronger aids like those, for example, for extended trot.

(7) *Raising the heels* Many riders acquire the bad habit of relying on the spur to produce even the simplest action from their horse such as moving from the halt into the walk. To do this they raise the heels and prod the horse's rib-cage with the spur. Inevitably the knee is also slightly raised and the seat weakened. The result is that the rider never acquires the instinctive habit of using the correct form of leg-aid without the spur, and from the very first moment that his horse moves he, the rider, is already wrongly positioned.

If he has to rely on the spur for those very simple movements, how much more will he feel the need to use it for greater effects? So he will come to use it all the time, and the horse will come to ignore any aid that does not include the spur. More and more, and particularly under stress, he will resort to this false use of the leg. The rider will gradually

FIG 8 **Incorrect forward-leg-aid**; leg drawn back behind the girth with dropped toe, raised heel and prodding spur.

debilitate himself and will never acquire a good and effective seat. Indeed, a sure sign of a good seat is the extent to which the rider's heel is seen to sink elastically with every aid and with every stride of the horse, the spur being reserved for very special or occasional use.

The cure for, or the means to avoid, this bad habit of raising the heels is threefold.

1 Ride without spurs, or as if you were not wearing them. Learn that the spur is not essential, and teach the horse to respond quickly and in full to the leg alone.

2 When riding with spurs make a conscious effort to keep them well away from the horse.

3 When it is essential to use the spur this should be done by keeping the heel down but turning the toe out so that the end of the spur is brought into contact with the horse by drawing it forward, from rear to front, against the lie of the hair, in the same way as the leg-aid itself is applied in a rear-to-front action (see next chapter). In this way the action of the spur is logically in accord with the action of the leg; it cannot bruise or hurt the horse; and will be accepted readily and without fear. Further, its use becomes nothing more than an

FIG 9 **Hands held too low**; below the straight line between bit and elbow. A bad fault.

extension of the normal leg-aid and therefore does not in any way disturb or weaken the seat.

(8) *Hands held too low* This is a much more serious fault than it may appear to be at first sight. The hands have no right to be below the elbow-bit line and, when they are, it is always the result of stiffness or tension in the arms or wrists, or in the hands themselves; a stiffness that will more or less inhibit the freedom of the horse's paces and the flow of muscular impulsion through his back. The hands will have become not only stiff but insensitive.

Because of the stiffness in the hands, the horse becomes reluctant to step freely into the bit. He feels that the rider is resisting him and will either fight that resistance by going above the bit, or he will avoid it by coming behind the bit. In either case his back will cease to swing and his paces will deteriorate, becoming relatively short, hurried and probably irregular.

It is easy to prove that low hands, that is to say hands that are below the line of elbow-to-bit, are stiff and more or less resistant. Assuming that the hands holding the reins are lying totally relaxed on the withers and with the thumbs uppermost they will, as the horse begins to take a continuous contact, be quite automatically pulled up by the reins into the straight-line position, the relaxed forearm having become merely an extension of the rein. Hold one end of a scarf or piece of string in one hand, and get someone to gently pull the other end . . . and see what happens.

If on the other hand the hands do not rise when the horse pulls the rein forward, it can only be that the rider himself is exerting a degree of muscular pressure to keep them down near the withers. He is doing the resisting, and the horse will dislike it and take avoiding action of some sort.

If the bit-elbow line is broken, the hands will not be able to give-and-take in an elastic manner when required; they will not be able to encourage the forwardness of the pace; and they will become harsh.

It is a lesser evil if the hands are held a little too high, above the line. That fault is not to be encouraged, but they will easily lower themselves from their own weight if permitted, and in the meantime they will at least be in self-carriage.

(9) *Twisted hands and bent wrists* Anyone wishing to shake hands with an elderly and delicate person will invariably lift their hand and make the approach with the thumb uppermost and with no tension in the forearm or the wrist. The wrists will not be bent either inwards or outward, nor will the fist be tightly clenched. He will do that instinctively because he knows that only in that manner can he shake hands delicately and sensitively. The rider's attitude to his horse's mouth should be exactly the same.

If the hands are turned so that their backs are uppermost [Fig. 10(b)], the two bones in the forearm will become crossed and tension will set in. It can be quite easily felt by the rider, and also by granny and the horse. The same tension will occur if the thumbs, despite being uppermost, are pressed forward and down [Fig. 10(e)], or if the little-fingers are pressed forward and upwards [Fig. 10(f)]. In either case the wrist will not be relaxed.

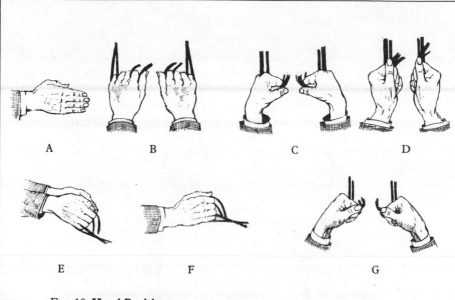

FIG 10 **Hand Positions**
(A) The gentle approach of shaking hands.
(B) Incorrect. Backs uppermost; fingers insufficiently closed.
(C) Incorrect. Wrists bent inwards, creating tension.
(D) Incorrect. Wrists bent outwards, creating stiffness.
(E) Incorrect. Wrists bent downwards, creating stiffness.
(F) Incorrect. Wrists bent upwards, creating stiffness.
(G) Correct. Thumbs uppermost. Straight line with forearm.

All these variations of hand faults are due either to ingorance or to carelessness. They can have very serious ill-effects on the horse's training and performance. They can be cured by determined self discipline.

(10) *Collapsing the back* The rider's back is collapsed when he has allowed the pelvis to tip or to rotate backwards over the seat bones to an extent that the slightly concave line to the loin is lost and replaced by a more or less convex line.

The rider sitting correctly is always trying to lengthen his body, to make himself taller, without stiffening but, as can easily be felt when sitting on a hard chair, the slightest convex rounding of the loin

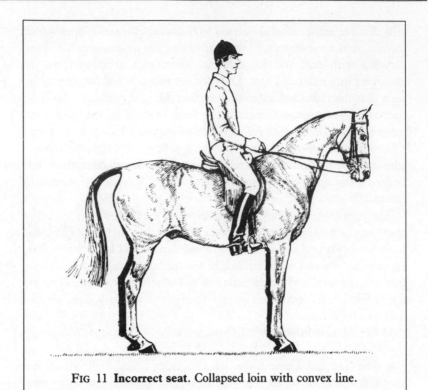

FIG 11 **Incorrect seat**. Collapsed loin with convex line.

immediately results in a shortening of the body; the rider can feel his head and eyes sinking.

To appreciate in more detail the adverse effects of a collapsed back it is necessary to remember that the forward positioning of the pelvis described at the beginning of this chapter has the highly important effect of ensuring that the lumbar portion of the spine is constantly in a position or shape from which it could act as a shock-absorber through the spring-like flexibility of the natural curve in the area. But that curve only exists effectively while the pelvis is in that particular posture. As soon as the pelvis begins to tip back, so the forward curve in the lumbar spine begins to straighten out, destroying the shock-absorber. The rider begins to bump and to inhibit the swing of the horse's back, to his own and his horse's discomfort.

It is not difficult for the rider to sit-up correctly, with the hipbones pressed forward (as for sitting-up at table) when the horse is standing still. Rather more effort is needed to maintain that position when in motion, and more especially when the rider is trying to urge his horse forward with seat and leg-aids into maximum impulsion as, for example, into extended trot. On such occasions it will frequently be seen that the rider has failed to maintain the pelvic position because he hasn't increased sufficiently the back-bracing action. He is no longer 'going along' with his horse in an easy and balanced manner. The loin, or small-of-the-back, has more or less collapsed and become rounded or convex instead of slightly concave. He will be slightly 'left behind', and will begin to grip with his thighs in order to remain in the saddle.

The inevitable corollary to the collapse of the back will be rounded shoulders, a hollow chest and a more or less drooping head. The rider loses his poise and the shock-absorbing capacity of his lower spine. He sits heavily and with his weight too far back, and in doing so he inhibits the swing of his horse's back. He will look lumpy, and no doubt feel lumpy to himself and to his horse. Eventually damage will occur to both backs.

Other adverse effects will follow, notably:

a The increased harshness of the rider's seat will affect his shoulders and subsequently his arms and hands, the latter also becoming harsh and inhibiting the horse's willingness to step forward into the bit with confidence. His back will already have become less supple and even hollow as the result of the rider's rougher seat.

b Because the increasingly vertical part of the lower spine will now be well behind the gravity line through the seat bones, the rider's weight will no longer be flowing down through his seat and into his heels. His weight will, to an increasing extent, be behind the movement of the horse and this will still further discourage the horse's back.

c The relative rounding of the rider's back will produce a connected rounding of the shoulders and a lowering of the head and neck, both of which will disturb the rider's, and consequently the horse's, balance.

To summarise, the collapse of the back is a very serious fault that acts contrary to the prime requirements of balance, suppleness, elegance, harmony and poise. The cure lies in the discipline of using the muscles of the loin to the extent that may be necessary according to the gait, speed and impulsion of the movement, to maintain the forward posture and pressure of the pelvis together with its tell-tale concavity of the lumber spine.

But here a word of warning must be given. Under no circumstances must the pelvis be tipped so far forward that the weight begins to come off the seat bones, or their forward edge, and be transferred instead to the muscles of the inner thighs or the crotch. That latter posture, which also puts the weight of the torso in front of the gravity-line through the seat bones, is indeed the much, and rightly, derided 'hollow back' seat, a label that cannot with any justice be applied to a rider whose spine is supple and who is correctly balanced with full weight on the forward edge of his seat bones . . . notwithstanding the desirable concavity in his loin.

And then there is a final warning about the danger of doing nothing. The rider's pelvis has to swing with the horse so that he 'goes along' with the movement and can sit quietly, smoothly, firmly and happily, undisturbed in the saddle. The pelvis has to swing, or rock, forward over its firm base on the front edges of the seat bones, and in the process make use of the flexibility and strength of the natural curve in the lower or lumbar spine. But that forward swing will not happen by itself, regularly and efficiently, unless the rider does something about it, to set it going and to maintain it. That something, that essential action, is the bracing of the back, the muscles of the loin; the thrusting forward of the hips and stomach into the hands; an action hardly visible but always happening; always supple but always positive. If the rider fails to make this action, if he does nothing, he will fail to 'go along' with his horse's movement; he will be, in effect, 'behind the movement'; he will have to grip with his thighs, if only very slightly; his back and loin will become increasingly stiff and his seat increasingly bumpy; he will flatten his horse's back; he will spoil his horse's paces. Those dangers, in that sequence are inevitable and unavoidable unless the rider acquires the knowledge and ability to *go along with the movement* by his own efforts. His back must be supple and his pelvis must move.

CHAPTER TWO

The Theory of the Aids

Part 1 FORWARD LEG-AIDS

THE RIDER'S LEGS constitute the riders's prime, and indeed virtually the only way of creating activity and motion from his horse. Once created, that motion can be controlled, modified, encouraged, guided, increased or generally adjusted by complementary action from one or more of the other forms of aid; but none of the latter can, of their own right, create the initial movement. Only the legs can do that. Much credit is invariably and rightly given to the power of the rider's seat to influence a horse in all manner of ways, but the seat alone is incapable of making a horse move, for example, from a halt into a walk, or from a walk into a trot; unless of course the horse has laboriously been taught some trick in which he has learnt to move forward whenever he feels a strange and curious positioning of the rider's seat bones; or whenever he hears his rider whistle the National Anthem. But such tricks are outside the scope of serious horsemanship.

Even the legs themselves achieve their results only somewhat indirectly through physical persuasion, and that persuasion is in the long run backed by the threat of sanctions from whip or spur. Every horseman knows that an obstinate or ill-trained horse will continue to stand still if he wants to, ignoring his rider's 'normal' aids of leg or seat. The most common and indeed universally used leg-aid in such circumstances, used even with some quite willing horses, is for the rider to deliver a series of more or less violent backward kicks with his heels against the horse's rib-cage. That is the aid taught to the child having his first donkey-ride when his mother cries 'kick him, darling'. There is no denying that such an aid does, more often than not, induce the animal to move, though probably only because he has found it too uncomfortable to stand still any longer and has learnt that the discomfort will cease if he moves. Such crude methods are of course inconceivable in intelligent equitation and are quite incapable of being developed into progressive finesse.

Progressive training must be geared and aimed at the concept of intimate harmony between the rider and the horse. True harmony implies that the two partners shall, as far as possible, think in harmony, feel in harmony and act in harmony. That is a very tall order and success will only be achieved, as in marriage itself, by the application of a great deal of intelligence, sympathy, understanding, forethought and mutual confidence. The rider, being the leader of the operation, is naturally responsible for the practice of all those qualities. Fear, discomfort and force (backward kicking legs), the very negation of sympathy and mutual confidence, will obviously have no place in the scheme of things.

In accordance with these principles it has been necessary to devise, over the centuries, the simplest and, to the horse, the most intelligible signal that he is required to go forward with lively energy. The rider's legs, which are always close to the horse and are very adaptable, are the obvious tools for the job, but the precise method of their usage requires a little more consideration. As with a kick, a straight squeeze has little logic in it for this particular purpose and can therefore quite easily result in confusion and frustration. Something better is needed and is available, and has long been accepted as the classical leg-aid.

When you wish to invite, or induce or encourage, another person to go through a doorway in front of you, it is unwise, and probably unproductive, to use your forefinger to prod that person in the ribs in a backward direction. The lady will probably flinch and step back with a look of strong distaste on her face. Far better, surely, and more natural, to use all the fingers to exert a light forward pressure on the rear part of her arm, or even her waist, supported perhaps by a mumbled verbal invitation. That message will invariably be understood and usually happily acted upon. No force. No discomfort. Message understood. Harmony reigns.

So it should be with the rider's leg and the horse. But since the leg cannot be placed behind the equivalent of the lady's arm or waist, the leg has to be used to exert a light inward-and-forward pressure on the most sensitive part of the horse's side and against, as it were, the lie of the hair. The essential logic lies in the slight but deliberately forward element of the pressure.

Since there is only such a slight mechanical logic about this aid, the horse will of course have to be taught to understand and respond to it. But because it is both psychologically and mechanically logical the horse will invariably learn the lesson extremely quickly and without any residual resistance. It should be taught from the very beginning of mounted work, assisted by the voice with which he is already acquainted and perhaps by light taps with the whip just behind the leg. He should never thereafter be allowed to forget the lesson or become careless in his response, and the rider must never lose the habit of using this form of leg-aid regularly and consistently.

It cannot be too often repeated that the basic leg-aid:

Begins with a bracing of the back;
Passes through the seat bones into the leg;
Is accompanied by a lengthening of the leg and a lowering of the heel.

Without those basic preliminaries it has little power.

The lengthening of the leg into the heel is a very important aspect of every leg-aid, if only because the longer the leg the more effective it is likely to be, other things being equal. But it is not only riders with long legs who can be good. Many with comparatively short legs are very good indeed because, in the long run, the seat and the loin play such a predominant part. In fact, it is how the legs act, rather than their actual length, that is significant.

If the legs appear to sink into the heel, it indicates that they are relaxed, are not gripping or being held up by the thigh muscles; and are not inhibiting the flow of weight downwards from the torso. It follows that the seat bones will be receiving the full flow of weight and the seat will accordingly be strong and, other things being equal, effective. By being relaxed, the legs are sensitive; and by being sensitive they can achieve their objective with minimum effort. If the rider, through his legs, is sensitive, the horse will remain sensitive and harmony between them will result. There is no escaping the constant interaction between horse and rider in all these matters, and that brings us back to the old motto that the rider can never excuse himself from blame when things do not go quite right.

A supple ankle and a lowering heel is a sure indication of the quality of a rider.

Part 2 UNILATERAL USE OF THE LEG

When both legs are used together in the manner described to urge a horse forward, the horse will respond by pushing himself forward more or less energetically by activity from his hindlegs. In such a case, the precise timing of the leg-stimulus in relation to the horse's stride is not very important. In fact it is better that the aids should be given more or less intermittently and not in-time with the stride because absolutely regular aids tend to become boring to the horse; to be accepted as inevitable; and eventually to be ignored as meaningless.

But within the general principle that legs act to stimulate the greater activity from the horse's hindlegs, there lies a deeper and much more subtle principle which mainly concerns the unilateral use of the leg, or those occasions when the desired effect can best be achieved by one leg only, or at least by only one leg at a time. That inner principle says that *a single leg-aid can only affect the hindleg on the same side.*

Here we come up against the not inconsiderable and purely mechanical effect of stimulation of the horse by the muscles of the rider's leg. When the leg acts on and stimulates the muscles of the horse's flank just behind the girth, they will also, by reflex action, stimulate the muscles that cause the stifle to flex and draw forward. For example, if the rider wishes, for some specific reason, to cause the right hindleg to operate more energetically and to engage further under the horse, he can only achieve that result by the use of his own right leg. His left leg can have no equivalent effect on the horse's right hindleg. It has to be his own right leg.

But then a further truth has to be understood if the aid is to act efficiently. *The horse can only respond to the leg-aid on the right side if it is applied while that hindleg is OFF THE GROUND, (in the air).*

If the aid is applied during the period when the hindleg is still on the ground it will be totally unable to respond because it is already busy carrying weight and has already determined the strength of its backward thrust.

If the hindleg has just reached the ground, or is just about to touch down, when the aid is applied, it will be too late for the horse to accept and digest the new idea in his brain and to make the necessary arrangements to adjust this action.

In either of these two latter cases the horse, frightened by his own inability to do what is asked of him but in an effort to do something, is likely to stiffen and flatten his back, thus destroying any chance of achieving additional engagement at the subsequent stride. There is therefore a danger involved in using a unilateral leg-aid unless the rider understands the matter and is able to feel with some accuracy his horse's strides; in other words, unless he has a firm, supple and balanced seat with which to do the feeling. However, this danger arises only when one-leg-aids are used to obtain forward movement from one hindleg. It does not arise when unilateral leg-aids are used to obtain lateral or more or less sideways movement from the horse (see Part 3) or for obtaining or encouraging a lateral bend in the horse's forehand.

Part 3 LATERAL LEG-AIDS

In order to make a horse move all or part of himself in a more or less sideways direction, the rider has little option but to act with his leg on the opposite side to the direction he wishes to take. He presses inwards instead of inwards-and-forwards, and that is another reason why the more normal aid for going forward should, in order to avoid confusion, always include that forward-pressing element that we have already stressed in Part 1 of this chapter.

The implication of a direct pressure or a tap from the rider's leg against the horse's side is much more readily understood by the horse than is the aid to go forward. The lesson is quickly learnt, and was indeed probably learnt in the stable long before he was asked to carry a rider on his back. It is such a very direct cause-and-effect affair that once learnt it seldom causes any further serious problems.

The precise position on the horse's side on which the pressure or tap is applied will vary, depending on exactly what the rider wishes to achieve and remembering that the normal position of the leg is somewhat in advance of central on the horse. For example:

a For a turn on the forehand, in which the horse has to move his hindquarters round his more or less stationary forehand, the rider's leg will need to be brought back to perhaps two hands-breadth, or six to eight inches, behind the girth to achieve effective influence over the quarters . . . and only the quarters.

b For a full-pass of ninety degrees to the side, as is possible in walk, the leg has to act on and influence the whole of the horse, the back and the front at the same time, and will therefore need to be only a little, say two or three inches, behind the normal position on the girth, i.e. approximately central on the horse's body.

c For a movement in which the forehand only is required to move more or less sideways, as for example in shoulder-in, the leg will be positioned well forward on the girth, perhaps a trifle further forward than normal.

It is clear from these three examples that the rider must always be able and ready to use each of his legs in a variety of positions in accordance with the requirements of the moment. And in that connection he must remain acutely aware of precisely *where* each of his legs are, both in relation to his horse and to each other. It would be futile and very confusing if, for example, the rider tried to obtain a right shoulder-in with his right leg held back in the position normally adopted for a left half-pass; a fault very often seen. But we shall be discussing such details in a later section. Here it must suffice to stress that in practice there will always be a number of differing positions for the lower-legs; that they will be changing with every change of gait, direction and movement; and that the rider must always be consistent in his methods if he is to avoid confusing his horse.

We must also mention here the fact that a lateral leg-aid can be used:

a Actively, to cause the horse to move away from it, or

b Passively, to control or prevent the horse from moving himself, or more usually a part of himself, towards the side on which the aid is applied. In other words, to prevent him moving against the leg.

In either case, the aid should be applied so as to include or engage the whole of the leg from the seat bone downwards, so that it will act to the greatest advantage with the least effort. And to ensure that the seat bone is playing its part, it is of great importance that the heel should be as low as possible, without any opening of the angle of the ankle even when the leg is drawn back.

It is a common fault to allow the angle of the ankle to open as the leg is drawn back for some lateral aid. It always weakens the seat and with it the effectiveness of the aid. The more the rider, in those circumstances, pushes his heel down towards the ground, the less far back will the leg need to be drawn; the less disturbance there will be to the rider's overall position; and the more effective will be the aid, whether active or passive, and particularly the part played by the seat itself. The seat bone and the heel will always complement each other, for better or worse.

Frequent reference has been made throughout these studies to the part played by the seat bones in the application of all leg-aids. They are the vitalising source of each leg-aid in that they are located at the operational end of the leg. Between them they carry the entire weight of the rider's torso which is restricted to just those two very small areas of bone. The pressure that they inevitably exert on the muscles of the horse's back is therefore very considerable and almost certainly much greater than most riders realise.

Admittedly the seat bones are cushioned from the horse's back by the padded panels of the saddle which must act to spread the weight over a wider area. But in practice the horse remains surprisingly sensitive to the nuances of pressure exerted by and through those two boney points. For example, a skilled rider on a reasonably well trained horse can perform tempi, and even one-time, flying-changes solely by the use of his seat bones and while holding his legs well away from any contact with the horse. A lady riding side-saddle, and without carrying a whip, can do the same thing, notwithstanding the fact that side-saddles have much thicker padding than cross-saddles. Both these examples illustrate the enormously important part played by the horse's back in his physical mechanism and arrangements. If the rider can control the back, which involves keeping it soft, supple and swinging from back to front, he can control the whole horse.

Part 4 THE DEEP SEAT

This discussion about the relation of the seat bones to the leg-aids is an appropriate moment to consider the real meaning of the commonly used and somewhat obscure phrase 'A Deep Seat'. Certainly it is universally accepted that a deep seat is a good thing. Everybody wants to have one and feels flattered if told that he has. Pupils are sternly told that they must sit 'deeper', though that instruction is very seldom accompanied by any useful advice as to how it can be achieved or what precisely it means. Most pupils are therefore left with no clear idea of what is expected of them. They struggle vainly to do something and in the process probably get stiffer and stiffer. It is worth finding out what is really involved.

The word 'deep' is itself to some extent misleading and confusing. Its validity is seen to be suspect immediately it is realised that its converse is 'shallow'. If a good and effective seat is deep, then a bad seat would be shallow. But nobody seriously uses the latter word. It would be meaningless.

A further point of confusion is that the pupils are frequently told that they must learn to sit 'in' rather than 'on' the saddle. But what can that possibly mean? Does one sit 'on' or 'in' a chair? And is it not the same thing anyway?

A saddle may have a soft seat, or the chair a cushion on it, but in either case the human being sits 'on' it with his full weight making the contact through the seat bones . . . provided he does not lean back onto his buttocks. *So long as he remains sitting upright*, he can do no other, though those seven qualifying words bring us close to the real point at issue. But meantime it can hardly be denied that a rider sitting correctly positioned in relation to his saddle at the halt or the walk will be just sitting 'on' the saddle, or 'in' it if you wish to use the more conventional term. But it makes no practical difference anyway, and it is certainly not within the rider's power to decide to sit either deeper or shallower.

So what does the instructor mean when he shouts 'sit deeper'? What is the real requirement for a good, elegant and effective seat on a horse? We have already discussed that in detail in Chapter 1, and may remember that it concerns primarily the continuous contact, at all gaits and in all circumstances, of the rider's weight through his seat bones with the surface of the saddle and therefore with the horse's back. The degree of weight must not be allowed to vary, except for some specific purpose and at the rider's discretion, because the horse will not be able to understand frequent variations of weight which invariably involve a degree of bumping and consequent discomfort.

There must be no bump. The seat bones must not leave, or tend to leave, and then return to the saddle. The piece of paper inserted between the seat bones and the saddle must remain there in trot and in canter, as in the walk.

What we are talking about is a seat which *remains firmly and softly in contact with the horse's back* at all speeds and gaits, with the legs relaxed and free to apply aids without disturbance to the primary seat itself. A firm and independent seat – independent of hands and legs.

Two things are absolutely fundamental to the achievement of such a seat: *a supple and relaxed spine, and relaxed legs that do not grip*. We are now back to the anology of the rope and the broomstick on the diving-board (page 19). That rope was not lying 'deep' on the board. It was just supple, soft and still on the board, and so must our seat be.

When the instructor says 'sit deeper', he is saying one or all of the following things:

a That the rider's seat is not firm enough. That he is actually bumping, i.e. being thrown up and out of contact with the saddle, and then falling back on to it with a bump.

b That the rider is failing to brace his back sufficiently to keep his pelvis in position and the shock-absorbing curve of the spine in operation.

c That the rider, by gripping with unrelaxed leg muscles, is preventing his weight from flowing fully into his seat bones and through them down into his heels.

The legs themselves have a great deal of weight, and it is their weight that above all will flow down into the heels and will act as a major steadying influence on the seat above them in the saddle . . . provided that the flow is not blocked or stifled by gripping.

In short, we need a seat that is genuinely firm in its contact with the saddle, and there are two visible signs that indicate when the rider is failing to sit in that manner. First, the distance between the rider's loin and the cantle of the saddle will fluctuate with every stride as his weight moves and falls behind the movement. The effect will be a visible and recurrent closing of the gap between loin and cantle. If the rider is truly 'going along' with the horse, the size of that gap will remain constant. Second, the loin becomes visibly stiff, immobile and harsh which in turn creates a jolting mobility of the shoulders which, in their turn, directly and adversely affects the softness and stillness of the hands.

The final sign of a good (deep) seat is that no movement appears to occur above the waist. Everything is absorbed in the area of the pelvis. The head and shoulders rest happily and at peace.

Part 5 WEIGHT AIDS

Undoubtedly the rider's weight plays an important part in the whole complex system of application of aids and of the rider's management and control of his horse. It cannot be otherwise since, from the moment the rider mounts, the horse will be acutely aware of and affected by his weight which he has to carry in a position designed to suit the rider rather than the horse. The rider must therefore consider very carefully what influence his none too stable weight will have on his horse's muscular ability and performance, and must be conscious of the fact that it is likely to be in a frequent state of flux and change. He will in any case be affecting his horse to approximately the same degree as a modest suitcase would be to a teenage child who was expected to carry it throughout his gymnastic class.

It is unwise, or even incorrect, to think of weight aids as being a system of aids in their own right, such as we ascribe to leg, seat or rein aids. The shifting of weight in the saddle can certainly be used to send messages when employed with sufficient consistency and frequency, but weight alone cannot apply any psychological or mechanical compulsion that the horse cannot ignore or overcome should he so wish. Further, the use of weight must never be allowed to disturb the horse's balance and must therefore be used with great discretion.

The use and influence of weight in riding is mainly and most profitably concerned only with its affect on the seat bones, those two points on which most of it is carried. The seat and the seat bones constitute the most valuable and variable aid at the rider's disposal, and any variation of weight on those bones is bound to have an immediate influence; one that will be easily recognised by the horse.

We have however to remember that the rider, in the interest of balance, has to sit very still with his seat bones located on one restricted area of the saddle. Any action of those seat bones has therefore to be restricted to pressing one of them a little more forward than the other; or putting a little more weight on one to increase its impact and relative influence on the horse; (*see* Aids for strike-off to canter page 62, or for the flying change of leg in canter page 89); or to strengthen the whole effect of a leg-aid when moving laterally. But in all these and similar uses of weight, it is the seat bones that constitute the aid and give the command, rather than the weight.

We should therefore consider the weight as being an aid to the aids of the seat, rather than an aid in its own right. The rider must of necessity use his weight all the time. His main concern will usually be to ensure that he uses it to the advantage, and not to the disadvantage, of his horse. He must keep his weight balanced and flowing in the direction of the movement.

Part 6 THE THEORY OF REIN-AIDS

The rein-aids are the most compelling and powerful of all the aids. They can do many things, but they cannot make a horse go faster or more forward. They can be helpful but also very harmful. With all these possibilities in mind, it is obviously desirable that every rider should study carefully their effects and potentialities for good or bad, and should fully understand how to use them for the best effect.

The first principle about the use of the reins lies in the fact that they may either guide or control the horse. And within the aspect of control, they should always be employed in one of three ways only. This is to say, they may either (a) allow, (b) restrain, or (c) oppose.

The second principle, which overlaps the controlling aspect and is perhaps the most important rule in riding, is that, without any qualification whatsoever, the reins *must never actually pull back*. Pulling backwards with the reins, under any circumstances, is to act against all the instincts of the horse; an action that he will invariably resent and resist, with deplorable results on his mind as well as on his physical well-being and his freedom of movement. Beginner riders may find this difficult to believe or accept, but they will assuredly come to appreciate it later on when and if they become good horsemen. They will therefore be well advised to accept from the start that every time they exert a distinct backward pull on their horse's mouth, even for a rein-back, they are doing some harm and starting a bad habit. This is discussed in more detail later on, in Chapter 6. But meantime you should remember:

a To restrain does not imply a backward pull.
b To oppose movement does not imply or need a backward pull.

The rider's hands can obviously exert innumerable variations of weight, pressure or direction on the reins and, through them, onto the horse's mouth. Sideways, upwards, downwards, backwards, and with one or both hands or reins, those variations will all have quite different and more or less compelling effects on the horse. As we have already noted, the effect of rein-aids is largely mechanical and compelling, whereas those of seat and legs are largely psychological with little if any assured compulsion. And just, or if only, because the reins are so unavoidably compelling, and because of their great variety, the rider should clearly have a clear and accurate idea of what all those variations are actually saying to the horse. It is by no means every rider who is always aware of precisely what his hands are doing all the time, or where they are positioned. Yet every time a hand moves, perhaps unconsciously, some sort of message will be communicated to the horse, and those messages may be, and often are, of a contradictory and confusing nature.

To provide riders with some guidelines towards ensuring that they use their hands and reins only in such ways as are logical and intelligible to the horse, rein-aids have long ago been classified into five main groups, known as the five Rein Effects. Within each of those five classifications there will be many slight variations available, but they will not alter the overall mechanical effect on the horse. The five Rein Effects, together with a visual description of the mechanical action on the horse, are shown in figure 12.

A *third principle* for the correct use of rein-aids is that no rein or hand action should ever be applied by itself or *without the prior application of a weight/seat/leg action originating from a bracing of the loin*. This means that the rein action only takes effect as the result of the horse pushing himself, in reaction to the seat and leg-aids, forward into the hand. Thus even the rein aid complies with the rule that all aids act from rear to front.

Rein-aids should always be applied with a minimal and usually invisible action of the hand. A slight turn of the wrist or a closing of

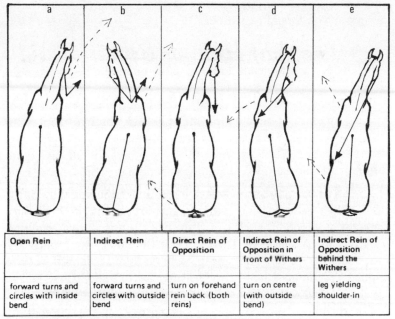

a	b	c	d	e
Open Rein	Indirect Rein	Direct Rein of Opposition	Indirect Rein of Opposition in front of Withers	Indirect Rein of Opposition behind the Withers
forward turns and circles with inside bend	forward turns and circles with outside bend	turn on forehand rein back (both reins)	turn on centre (with outside bend)	leg yielding shoulder-in

Note: Solid line and arrow indicates direction of rein effect.
Dotted line and arrow indicates direction of consequent movement of the horse.

FIG 12 **Rein Effects.**

the fingers on the rein is all that should be necessary. The horse is very sensitive, and nowhere more sensitive than in its mouth to slight adjustments to the rein or bit. The rider's hand must be in quiet harmony with the horse's delicate mouth.

CHAPTER THREE

The Half-Halt, or Universal Aid

IT MAY SEEM anomalous to insert this chapter on the aids for the half-halt before dealing with the aids for putting the horse into some form of motion. He is still at the halt. But we should soon find ourselves in trouble if we tried to do it the other way round. We cannot in practice apply the aids for walk-on from a halt until we have applied a preliminary half-halt. The latter has to be done first, and so we should deal with it first on paper.

To explain that apparent anomaly in more detail, the action of the preliminary half-halt, important before virtually all aids and quite essential before the move-off from a halt, can be likened to stepping into a car and switching on the current. It is not a bit of good putting the car into gear or expecting the engine to turn over until that essential preliminary has been carried out. Without it, nothing useful can happen. The electrical connection has to be made.

So it is with riding. Before he can do anything useful, the rider must first make the connections within himself and between himself and his horse. Both must be switched on and alerted. Both must be warned and prepared that something is to follow. Then and only then can the message, in the form of an aid for something specific, pass smoothly through the system to produce the desired result, and without being at some point stifled, blocked or ignored. There will then be harmony and understanding.

THE AIDS FOR THE HALF-HALT

Article 408 of the F.E.I. Rules for Dressage defines the half-halt in the following terms. It is 'a hardly visible, almost simultaneous

FIG 12A **The Half-Halt.** Powerful and correct use of rider's back, pushing the horse forward into the hand to obtain balance and collection. The hands do not move and do not pull back.

coordinated action of the seat, the legs and the hand of the rider . . .' That is quite correct as far as it goes, but it fails to give any assistance on the first question that the pupil needs to ask, i.e. *What action?* We will try to fill that gap.

To apply a half-halt the rider must:

a Brace his back, thereby fractionally pushing the top of his pelvis forward and putting just a little more tension into his lower or lumbar spine which will in turn slightly increase the downward-and-forward pressure of the seat bones on the muscles of the horse's back. In doing this he will be saying to the horse 'I am here. Pay attention.'

b In conjunction with the bracing action in **a**, he will lengthen his legs into his heels and simultaneously close them more firmly onto the horse. He will thus also say to the horse 'listen, and feel me'. There will need to be sufficient forwardness in the leg-aid (see Chapter 2) to

53

put the horse at least mentally forward into the hand or bit, even if he is not required to make any movement of his feet. To change the analogy from the motor-car, there must be just a little steam in the boiler, or wind in the sail of the boat.

c Almost, if not quite, simultaneously with the pelvic and leg action, he will close his fingers more firmly on the reins, while keeping his elbows steady and close to his sides, to increase the rein tension just sufficiently to prevent or restrain the horse from responding to the legs with an unwanted degree of forwardness. But should that occur, the hand must NEVER pull back, and that is assisted by the light contact between the elbows and the sides.

d The final and vital action of all half-halts is that of release. The coordinated actions of loin, seat, legs and hand must never be held on or become fixed. Fixation in the rider will invariably produce a reaction of fixation in the horse that would inevitably destroy the desire and the ability to 'go forwards' that we must always try to foster. If a half-halt fails to produce the required response, however slight that may be, it must be released and repeated, released and repeated, until success is achieved.

Those four aspects cover the essential half-halt in its basic form, in which it is used, in the words of the F.E.I. Rules, 'to increase the attention and balance of the horse' and also, to be sure, of the rider himself.

The degree of strength, tension or direction that the rider puts into the actions of back, seat, leg and hand will naturally vary according to the circumstances of gait, balance and speed from which the half-halt is called. In every case it will be followed by further aids for some specific movement, change of direction or gait. In each case the half-halt aids will have been distinct, hardly visible, almost simultaneous and coordinated, or inter-dependent. No part can be effective without the rest.

To summarise the theory and practice of this most subtle and vital of all dressage training principles, we may say that the half-halt is used:

a To increase or improve the attention and balance of the horse at any time when such improvement may seen desirable . . . and that means very frequently.

b To precede, in a preparatory manner, the execution of any movement or of a transition to lesser or higher paces or to different gaits. In this respect it acts in exactly the same manner as does the voice of the drill-sergeant when he shouts 'Squa-a-a-d' before giving his order for the squad to halt, to form-fours, or to come to attention.

In practice, the half-halt cannot be effective, or cannot even happen at all within the horse, no matter what the rider may do or what aids he may give, unless the horse is soft and supple in the back, neck and poll, and is in at least reasonable control of his own balance. Unless those essential prerequisites exist, the horse will be physically incapable of responding in the desired manner to the very subtle aids involved. If those aids are met by muscular resistance due to stiffness or severe imbalance, they will be killed stone dead as they would be if applied to a heavy baulk of timber, and the sensitivity of the horse will begin to deteriorate.

It is for that reason that, except in a most elementary form, the half-halts should not be brought into the training schedule until the horse has become well established in the first training phase, that is to say until he can be ridden consistently in all three gaits in rhythm, with contact and with *Losgelassenheit* (i.e. the horse is supple and loose and completely free from tension). To try to teach the half-halts before that time is to risk lasting damage and ultimate failure.

When it is time to bring half-halts into the schedule, it must be done with great gentleness, patience and sensitivity. The rider must be watchful and ready to feel the slightest indication that his horse has understood and reacted correctly with his back and poll, and must then immediately relax the aids to express his appreciation. It is vital that that reward be given, or else the horse will come to think that the quite demanding aids are just a nuisance and have little useful purpose as far as he can see.

Gradually, very gradually, more and more can be asked by more demanding aids, though the aids must always yield in the end and before they become heavy and dead. That is one golden rule that must never be forgotten. Every half-halt must end, before it is too late, with a clear yielding of the restraining rein-aid. Failure to do that will lead to an ever increasing resistance right through the horse.

THE HALF-HALT EFFECT

When the half-halt is given to a horse on the move in any of the three gaits, its main effect and purpose should be to cause the horse to improve the engagement of his hind legs and to push himself that much more forward into the rider's restraining hand, thus shifting more weight onto the quarters to the benefit of the lightness of the forehand and the overall balance. From this it will be seen that forward driving aids of the seat and legs may need to be quite strong although the hands, it must again be stressed, must never be pulled-back or be held on. They must be quickly released.

The employment of half-halts should not only be thought of as linked with the beginning of certain specific movements, which indeed they are, but also as an almost never-ending activity to engender and maintain the best possible performance from the horse in all his basic paces. No horse, however well trained, can be expected to operate to perfection, or even to his highest potential, indefinitely and of his own accord. He cannot be put into a certain gear with a fixed setting of the accelerator and left there to get on with the job while the rider does nothing. There is nothing in his mentality that would encourage him to behave like that, or even to understand the objective. He has therefore to be 'ridden' up to the mark all the time, a fresh supply of stimulating energy being injected by the rider with virtually every stride. And the tools with which the rider does that are the half-halts, subtle and hardly visible but felt, constantly correcting the rider's own position and the horse's position and output.

As the rider becomes more adept and skilfull with his half-halts, they will increasingly be found to merge into the aids for each specific gait and for each specific movement that follows the half-halt, to the extent that, in the end, the half-halt itself will become the aid for the movement. This we shall be considering in the following chapters.

But how, it may be asked, can a rider know for certain whether his horse has responded satisfactorily to the half-halt aids? He has asked for almost nothing, yet he must get something in return. So precisely what does he expect?

The answer can be stated clearly enough. As a direct and immediate response to his aids, the rider should experience two faint but quite distinct sensations:

1 A slight rounding or lifting of the horse's back-muscles as the quarters engage and the horse prepares himself for action. The back rises to the rider's seat and the horse says 'Yes, I am with you'.

2 A slight softening of the poll and the jaw, felt in the fingers and indicating that the horse is offering no resistance to the bit, though pushing himself up to it; is not leaning on it; and is waiting and ready for guidance. The horse says 'I am cooperating, and will take you anywhere.'

With those sensations, the rider will believe he is in heaven and will be able to do many marvellous things.

CHAPTER FOUR

Aids for Specific Gaits and Transitions

Part 1 AIDS FOR WALK-ON FROM HALT

a Alert the horse with a minimum half-halt which will correct the rider's position and establish mutual communication and balance.

b Apply stronger driving aids of seat and legs, the latter both together on the girth with sinking heels and with a forward-and-inward direction. Do not hold the aid too long. Repeat more strongly with the legs if necessary but with quick, repeated pressures which in turn, if the horse remains sluggish, should be supported by a light tap from the whip immediately behind the rider's leg. Every horse must be trained to respond immediately to this simplest of all aids.

Both legs act together and in the same manner to ensure that the horse moves forward on a straight line. Once the walk has been established, the leg-aids may be used alternately to encourage the forward swing of each hindleg in turn (see Chapter 2, Part 2).

To improve freedom of stride in walk, the aids are best applied every stride, first the right and then the left, as the hindleg on that side is in the air. The rider can check the correctness of this timing by watching the foreleg or shoulder. As the left foreleg is moving back, the left hindleg will be moving forward in the air, and that is the time to apply the left leg-aid. The same rule applies to the right side.

58

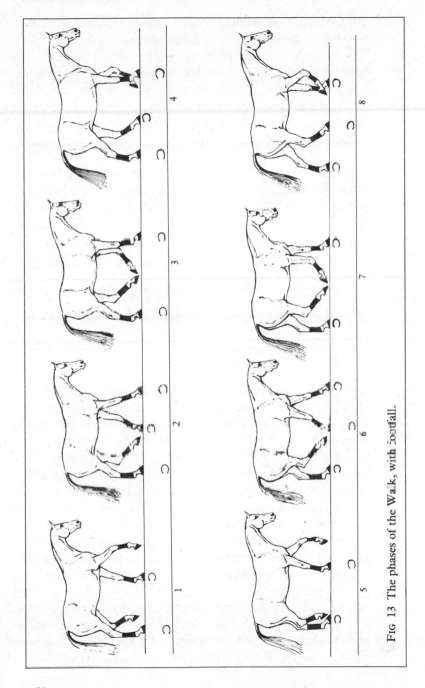

FIG 13 The phases of the Walk, with footfall.

The riders's leg should not visibly move, but bracing the loin may be strongly developed into a visible action.

c The hands yield sufficiently, as soon as the horse is felt to be moving, to allow him to go forward confidently, but not so much that contact will be lost. The amount of yielding by the hands, and the length of rein allowed, must be adapted to the type of walk intended, either free, extended, medium or collected.

The hands retain the contact, a very light movement of the wrists taking care of the movement made by the horse's head and neck in the more collected variations of the gait. The whole arm may move to follow the increased movement in the extended variation.

Part 2 AIDS FOR THE TROT-ON, FROM HALT (Sitting trot)

a Alert the horse with a half-halt that is a little stronger than for the walk-on, which will correct the rider's position and establish the mutual communication and balance.

b Apply two or three quick vibrating driving aids with both legs (inward and forward with lowering heels) simultaneously, with strong bracing of the loin, but without allowing the legs to lose contact with the horse, the action being entirely within the boot. This combined action amounts to a very active half-halt.

The distinction between the aids for the walk-on and the trot-on lies in the fact that, for trot-on, the horse has to be made to use much more energy in order to lift himself off the ground and into the characteristic hopping gait of the trot in which he springs alternately from one diagonal pair of legs to the other with a moment of total suspension between each hop or step. To do this he needs to be a little more collected, his weight more evenly balanced between the fore and hind quarters, to give himself the power to push himself upwards off the ground for the first and each subsequent little jump. His overall frame will be a little shorter and therefore the rider's hand/rein aids will need to exercise a firmer restraining influence than they did for the walk-on, although they must still allow the muscle action to flow from the back through the neck. In the walk gait the horse never has less than one forefoot and one hindfoot on the ground at any one moment (see Fig. 13) and consequently has little difficulty in maintaining balance. To assist in maintaining balance into the trot, the rider must never allow his torso to lead his pelvis. The pelvis must always lead.

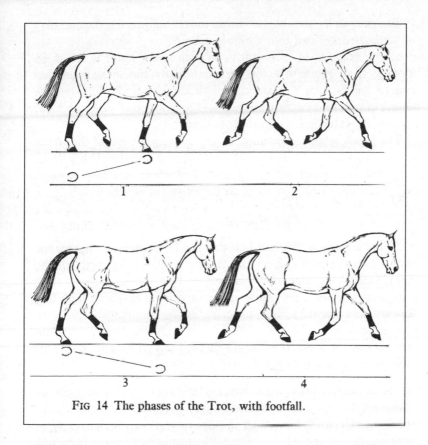

FIG 14 The phases of the Trot, with footfall.

Once the trot has been established, it is then maintained by frequently repeated half-halts of similar kind, though it will be necessary, when riding 'in position' on a straight line or on a curve or circle, to apply a stronger aid with the inside loin/seat/leg than the outer one, to keep the horse correctly bent and/or flexed round the rider's inside leg. And as always, the heel should sink a little with each application of the aid. This latter point will occur only if the loin is properly braced forward and the legs remain hanging in a natural and relaxed manner without tensing or gripping. Since in trot there is virtually no movement of the horse's head or neck, there should be absolutely no visible movement in the rider's hands except in so far as is necessary to make some occasional and specific adjustment to the posture or direction of the horse.

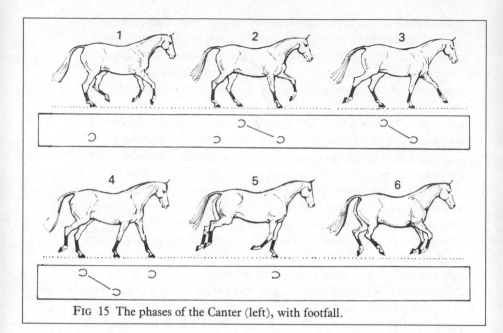

FIG 15 The phases of the Canter (left), with footfall.

Part 3 AIDS FOR CANTER-ON, FROM HALT, WALK OR TROT (to canter-left)

a Alert the horse with a half-halt, to correct rider's position and establish mutual communication and balance.

b The aid for canter should be thought of and given in two distinct but closely related parts that flow smoothly from the one into the other:

1 By unilaterally bracing the right loin for the left canter, apply extra pressure onto the right seat bone and into the right heel. That primary action will induce the horse, in order to carry the extra weight on that side, to do so with his right hindleg, the leg that must initiate the canter-left. If he is already in motion, he will try to do this by stepping a little further under himself with that leg, just to help himself. The use of the seat bone in this manner and for this purpose will largely obviate the excessive movement of the rider's right (outside) leg to the rear, with all its dangers of making the horse crooked, that is so frequently seen and which so often becomes unsightly. That big-swing to the rear also has the undesirable effect of

reducing the amount of weight on the seat bone just when we want to increase it. But here once again we should try to remember that the correct and most efficient action of the seat bone is assisted by pushing the heel down towards the ground and reducing to a minimum any rearward swing of the lower leg. This outside leg has very little else to do apart from keeping contact and maintaining impulsion. It should not push against the horse's side. It is however misleading to think that the action of the outside or right seat bone and leg will of itself induce a left canter strike-off. It prepares the horse for the positive strike-off aid following as in (2) below.

2 Strongly brace the left side of the loin to push forward the left hip and seat bone in conjunction with the full inward-and-forward leg-aid on that side, pressing forward onto the girth and lengthening the leg down into the heel. This is the signal and the encouragement to the horse to jump forward, off the well grounded right leg (see 1 above) into the second and third beats of a canter stride.

The power and the effectiveness of this pushing action comes from the combined use of the seat bone pressing forward onto its front edge, and the fully employed lower leg, both of which encourage the horse to bend and become somewhat concave on that side and so to facilitate the adoption of the natural posture for the canter-left. Both the seat pressure and the leg pressure should be somewhat held-on, or prolonged, in their action to allow time for the horse to lift himself and to find the relatively slow tempo of the canter gait, as compared with the walk or trot that will have preceded it.

To summarise so far this double-action of the seat (and legs) for the canter-on, strike-off as it is more usually called, we use first the right loin-and-seat bone and then the left loin-and-seat bone, in very quick succession, for a canter-left; and vice versa for the canter-right. It may need a little practice to get the timing and harmony right, but it's logical and efficient, and the rider will reap the benefit.

c The reins act in their turn in a restraining manner to encourage the horse to respond to the overall half-halt-and-jump aids by pushing himself forwards and upwards, rather than just forwards, to achieve the extra elevation of the forehand demanded during the first phase of the canter. The inside hand should remain as soft as possible at first to encourage flexion to the inside, and must then quickly and generously release all restraint in order to allow the horse the freedom to step confidently forward with a longer stride into the third or leading-leg beat of the first full canter stride.

Throughout the whole process, it is of overriding importance that the rider should use his back, strongly but always supply, in such a way that pushing forward the hipbones (top of the pelvis) ensures that the pelvis as a whole *always leads the torso*. The torso should not lean back behind the balance-line, but should be drawn or carried forward by the action of the pelvis below it. The effectiveness of all the aids will be defeated if the torso is allowed to creep in front of the seat bones.

The aids described above remain in general the same whether the canter is asked for from the halt, the walk or the trot. It is only the timing that varies, being somewhat slower and more prolonged in the halt and walk, and rather quicker but not hurried from the trot.

The rider must remember that, from the walk and the trot, the actual transition into the canter gait can only be made by the horse from his new outside hindleg. He must make the effort as that leg comes to the ground and the rider must time his aid-sequence to that moment (see **b** (1) and (2) above). But he must also remember (see Chapter 2, Part 2), that each leg-aid must be applied when the hindleg on the same side is actually in the air, or else it cannot be effective.

The ideal moment to apply the aids for Walk to Canter Left is therefore as shown in Fig. 13.6.

The ideal moment to apply the aids for the transition Trot to Canter Left is as shown in Fig. 14.3.

Part 4 AIDS FOR CANTER TO TROT

a Maintain or improve the quality of canter, keeping the horse fully on the aids, by the usual series of small half-halts given at every stride when the leading foreleg is on the ground and the leading hindleg is in the air, and so able to respond by reaching a little further forward to engage more energetically and improve the impulsion into the hand and the thrust for the next stride.

b Apply two or three strong half-halts in preparation for:

c One strong half-halt on the stride when the transition to trot is required. This will include a stronger though momentary opposing effect from the hands, not allowing but definitely not pulling back, and more from the outside than the inside rein. This rein-aid will slightly shorten and confirm the diagonal footfall of the second beat (Fig. 15.3) of the canter stride (also required for the trot) and slightly delay the fulfilment of the third beat onto the leading leg (Fig. 15.4). The latter delay will allow time for the outside hindleg to catch-up with it and so form the second and essential diagonal of the trot (Fig. 14.3).

The ideal moment for this strong half-halt will be seen in Fig. 14.2. The horse has provided one diagonal (from the preceding canter). The rider must achieve the second into trot.

d As the second diagonal is achieved, the rider immediately applies a final and very positive forward half-halt to drive the horse forward into a full trot rhythm without any intervening 'dribbling' steps. His seat must be firm and sensitive enough to catch the moment to make the transition clear, smooth and forward. In phases b, c, and d, both legs must act together on the girth; the seat bones equally weighted and parallel, for the trot.

Finally, the inside hand must re-establish softness on that side.

Part 5 AIDS FOR CANTER TO WALK

a Maintain and improve the canter by half-halts as above for canter to trot.

b Apply two or three strong half-halts with the object of engaging the quarters so that they will carry more weight and make it easier for the horse not to fall on his forehand when the moment comes to reduce, within only one stride, the speed of his progress from canter to the very much slower gait of walk. He must be prepared for that sudden reduction of speed, and so must the rider.

c Apply a final strong half-halt when the initiating hindleg touches the ground in what the rider wishes to be the last full canter stride.

To understand just what must now happen, study and compare the footfall sequences shown in figure 15, phases 1 and 2 (canter-left), and figure 13, phases 4, 5, and 6 (walk). The half-halt, having been timed on the right hindleg in canter-left, will come through to be effective as the subsequent right diagonal grounds. The horse then, and for a moment, is easily balanced with three feet on the ground (Fig. 15.2) in a posture that corresponds almost exactly with the phase 4 of the walk (Fig. 13.4). By prolonging the whole half-halt effect for an instant while the horse slows down into the walk phase 3, instead of the very similar canter-phase 3 (Fig. 15.3), the rider can then gently release the horse into the subsequent walk phases by easing the restraint on the reins.

d As soon as he has taken the first step forward into the walk sequence, the rider urges him forward into the required length of stride by applying alternate leg-aids in the normal manner for that gait.

N.B. The key to successs in this transition lies in the achievement of really good collection and balance immediately before the transition is demanded. The similarities of the footfall, as noted in **c** above, render it a relatively easy transition for the horse to execute smoothly.

Part 6 AIDS FOR CANTER TO HALT

This is a very difficult transition. The rider must not expect the impossible and should therefore study carefully what is possible

a Several strong half-halts for two or three strides before the point of halt, to prepare and collect the horse; to engage the quarters; to shorten the stride; and to reduce the momentum.

b A final and still firmer half-halt, amounting almost but not quite to a full-halt, just as the leading leg of the last full canter stride touches the ground; say the left foreleg in the canter-left (see Fig. 16.2). This aid, of loin/seat/leg/hand, must effectively retain that leading foreleg on the ground until after the next or initiating hindleg has grounded once more, thus cutting-out the usual moment of suspension (Fig. 16.3 and 4). Compare with Fig. 15.4, 5, and 6.

The severe slowing down, or holding in position, of the forehand will result in the right (initiating) hindleg coming further forward and more directly under the centre of gravity than usual, as the horse endeavours to obey the restricting aids that were given in phase 4.

c The strong half-halt will be slightly released as the right-diagonal legs come forward, the right foreleg passing the left (Fig. 16.5), which by that time is at the rearmost point of its grounding, but going

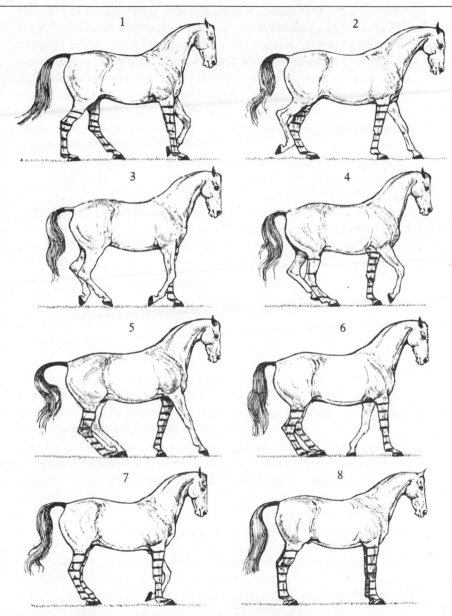

FIG 16 Left-Canter to Halt. Note main half-halt applied at (3). Weight carrying legs hatched.

less far forward than its normal stride would have taken it. The left hindleg will ground square, or almost square, with the well advanced right hindleg (phase 7).

   d The final closing of the hands for the full-halt is applied as the horse allows his body to sway forward over the slightly advanced left foreleg, and as the right foreleg steps up beside the former into a square halt, (Fig. 16.7 and 8). That final step forward with the front leg is necessary to allow sufficient room for the body between the front and back feet.

   e All aids are now gradually released, but contacts maintained for immobility.

CHAPTER FIVE

Aids for Lateral Movements

Part 1 GENERAL

THERE ARE FOUR basic forms of lateral movement, the Leg-Yield, the Shoulder-In, the Travers and the Half-Pass. We need not concern ourselves here with the many and various elaborations on those basic themes that can be developed and used in training sessions or displays, since the aids for them will remain virtually unchanged for each main type. The variations usually concern the main types being performed on circles or curved lines instead of on straight lines.

It is as well to start this study of lateral aids by remembering that, although their logic may be quite simple and certainly clear enough to be fairly easily understood by any intelligent and sensitive horse, it is only the rein-aids that contain any mechanical compulsion in their action. But even so, a glance at the drawings of the basic forms in Fig. 17 makes it abundantly clear that the reins alone will not suffice to produce, satisfactorily and consistently any of those movements. In each case they play an essential part as we shall see when we study the details, but in each case they have to be supported and complemented by the weight, seat and leg aids. And since, as we have said, those latter aids can enforce no mechanical compulsion, their effectiveness can only be the result of careful and intelligent training in the early stages of a horse's career.

Later on, the rider should beware of the temptation to use pseudo-forceful aids such as, for example, the continuous or too frequent use of whip or spur to achieve his lateral objectives. If such unnatural aids seem to be required it will be because he has allowed his normal or natural aids to become slipshod or the horse to become inattentive. But by resorting to spur or whip, other than gently and on rare or

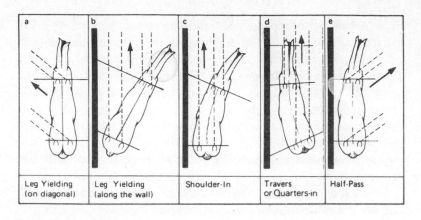

| Leg Yielding (on diagonal) | Leg Yielding (along the wall) | Shoulder-In | Travers or Quarters-in | Half-Pass |

---------- footsteps

——————— angle from track

arrow indicates direction of movement

FIG 17 Basic Lateral Movements.

exceptional occasions, he will be starting down a long and slippery slope from which it will be increasingly difficult to extricate himself. He would be better advised to go back to square-one and to repolish the basic training by which the horse is first taught, and then maintained like a well tuned violin, to respond habitually and willingly to very light aid touches and pressures.

When the light leg-aids have constantly to be supported by the spur, it is a clear indication that the normal system of communication, based on intelligence and mutual cooperation, has broken down and is in need of repair. To put it briefly, the rider is riding badly.

Part 2 AIDS FOR LEG-YIELDING

Leg-yielding can be practised in all three gaits; first in the walk; later and more frequently in the trot; and less usually in the canter. It can be ridden not only along straight lines, but on circles and curves, the aids being virtually the same.

The Aids for Leg-Yielding (on Four Tracks) to left, Fig. 17.a and b

a A half-halt for several successive strides in the existing gait to alert and balance the horse; to perfect the rider's position; and to harmonise the partnership.

70

b A half-halt to put the horse into the correct position for a leg-yield, for example to the left, that is to say to put him straight in body and neck but with a slight right-flexion at the poll only, or away from the direction in which he will be asked to travel. The horse should now be firmly on-the-aids with contact on the left or outside rein predominant over the right.

c Sink the right heel and apply the right leg-aid slightly behind its normal position on the girth, so that it will act to influence the whole horse rather than on either the front or the back end alone (see Chapter 2, Part 3).

The left or outside leg remains on the girth and should be used only lightly but sufficiently to keep the horse working with impulsion up to the bit.

The action of the right or inside leg will be mainly lateral, directly against the side of the horse, but may have to assist the other leg with a degree of forward action, without altering its location, should the horse tend to lose impulsion.

d The rider must sit straight in the saddle, his shoulders and hips at right-angles to the horse's spine, and without collapsing either hip. However, it is important that a full share of the weight be maintained on the left seat bone to make the leg fully operative in its job of maintaining impulsion. He must also ensure that his weight really does move to the left in harmony with the horse's sideways or diagonal movement. He must not let it slide to the inside over the dominant right leg.

e The outside or left rein is opened slightly to take the horse away into the sideways direction. A turn of the thumb outwards should be sufficient. The right or inside rein complements the action and the effect of the left rein by acting 'in opposition' to the directly forward movement, in the direction 'behind the wither' and toward the rider's left hip. The right hand must not on any account cross the line of the neck. This is an example of the use of the fifth rein-effect (see Fig. 12e (page 51)), and assists the overall leg-yield by exerting a slight but definite mechanical influence on the horse to move away to the left.

f When the movement is completed, or if the horse falters in his rhythm or impulsion, the rider drives him forward with strong half-halts to set him onto his new course or to put him back onto the aids.

N.B. the horse will presumably have been given his preliminary lessons in obedience to lateral aids in the stable, or when he was being led in-hand, before he was ever backed.

Part 3 THE AIDS FOR SHOULDER-IN (on Three Tracks) Fig. 17c

When riding a shoulder-in it must never be forgotten that we expect the quarters and hindlegs to remain square on the original track, so that the hind feet will continue to move straight along their original alignment with no twist in the loin or crossing of the legs. The hind toes will continue to point straight forward along the track (see Fig. 17c).

It is only the forehand, or that part of the horse which is forward of thoracic vertebra number 13, which is roughly the point on which the rider sits, that has to be bent and brought inwards and onto a parallel but overlapping track, the bend in that part of the horse right up to the poll being smooth and continuous. But because the bend has its base and its beginning on an otherwise straight spine, the amount of bend shown in the shoulder-in or in any other similar posture will gradually increase as it gets further from its starting point at T13.

It is important to keep that picture in mind because the aids we have to apply must be precisely geared to achieve just this somewhat intricate result. The aids themselves have to be correspondingly accurate and capable of subtle adjustment according to the response and ability of the horse. It is a completely different problem when compared with for instance asking the horse to trot forward out of a walk.

So we will begin, for a right-shoulder-in:

a Two or three half-halts to establish position, balance and impulsion, with special note of the need to have the horse lightly flexed and soft on the inside rein, the latter point being perhaps the key to the whole exercise.

b Lead the forehand off the track to the right as if beginning, or maybe continuing, a large circle. It is easiest, but not essential, to do this immediately after reaching the track on the completion of a circle or corner.

As the opening right rein-aid is given (Fig. 12a) to direct the horse towards the inside of the track the right hipbone, followed by the right seat bone, must be pressed forward by a unilateral bracing of the loin on that side to initiate a strong and forward leg-aid that will result in a lowering of the right heel as it presses inward-and-forward on the girth. Since the main purpose of this inside leg-aid is to encourage the horse to move his forehand, and only his forehand, away to the left on an alignment parallel to the hindfeet on their original track, it is imperative that the right lower-leg should not be drawn back behind the girth, a fault that is often seen when a rider is afraid that his horse will not move sufficiently sideways. Such a position is however totally illogical and even harmful to our purpose as it inevitably tends to push the quarters out and thus cause the beginning of a tendency to leg-yield (instead of shoulder-in) with the hindlegs crossing instead of remaining straight forward. To repeat, only the forehand is required to move laterally, and it follows that the rider's inside leg-aid must speak only to the forehand and not to any other part of the horse. Further, if it is applied correctly on the girth, it will be operating on the only area in which the horse is capable of bending round it, bearing in mind that the horse cannot bend at all in its main rib-cage.

c As the forehand begins to come off the original track to form the three-track mode of progression, the left rein is opened firmly and for a moment to lead the horse along the line of the track, indicating to him that he is not after all going to continue along the circular or bent alignment to the right. That left rein-aid is held only momentarily and is then brought quietly back, without loss or change of contact, to its normal position in which, as the outside rein, it will lie lightly against the outer curve of the bent neck, to control that bend and provide the main contact with the bit. The horse is then ridden into that contact by the right or inside seat/leg-aid.

d The rider's left or outside leg should be in action from the beginning of the movement and drawn back a little behind the normal position on the girth, the toe being kept well to the front throughout.

In the first place, as the horse is bent into the preliminary corner or curve, and is led off the track with his forehand, the outside leg lies passively against the horse to assist him to bend round the rider's inside leg and to prevent the hindlegs falling outwards from the true track. Strength is only required if the rider feels that there is a tendency for the quarters to fall out; otherwise the leg should be purely passive. Indeed, considerable care should be taken to ensure that this outside leg does not push the quarters to the inside of the track of the forelegs. This aspect will be facilitated if the toes are kept well to the front and consequently the spur well away from any, perhaps unconscious, contact with the horse.

Once the shoulder-in begins, which is much more difficult for the horse than moving on a curve, the outside leg-aid should act a little more positively to ensure that the quarters do not escape from the somewhat difficult alignment of the movement by falling outward and so beginning to twist away from their important squareness on the track. A line drawn through the hips must be retained at right-angles to the track. If that squareness is lost, the horse's inside hindleg will no longer be flexing forward towards his centre of gravity, that being one of the main objects of the exercise.

Despite its position somewhat further back than normal, the outside leg may be required, in addition to its primary job of containing the quarters, to assist the inside leg in maintaining impulsion by acting forwards as well as inwards, albeit without changing its rearward location on the horse. Some degree of this combined leg-action is usually necessary to keep the horse working forward into the hand and thus to maintain the length and rhythm of the stride which can otherwise very easily be lost.

Part 4 AIDS FOR TRAVERS (on Three Tracks)

This is the easiest of all the lateral movements, for the simple reason that the horse continues to move his limbs more or less exactly in the direction in which his head is pointing. The line of impulsion therefore coincides very closely with the line or direction of movement, which is not so with other lateral work.

When riding the travers, the rider must feel and ensure that the horse's head remains pointing and aligned straight along the original track. There will be a relatively slight bend throughout the neck and forehand, becoming steadily less and eventually terminating as it approaches the point where the rider sits, approximately over vertebra T13, and this will bring the line through the shoulders only a little out of square with the track. The quarters, at the tail-end of the spine that is straight from behind T13 will be brought inside the main track to the extent that the outside hind foot follows directly in the steps of the inside forefoot. In that position, the forelegs proceed straight down the original track with only a virtually indiscernible tendency to cross the outside over the inside one while the hindlegs, the outside crossing over the inside one, will be moving along their parallel and overlapping track with a slight sideways swinging action from the hips (see Fig. 17).

The travers is an easier movement for the horse to perform and for the rider to execute than the shoulder-in if only because the horse's head remains on the direct alignment of his movement and consequently it is easier to keep him moving forward and up to the bit. However, that advantage is counterbalanced by the fact that the hindlegs are not moving straight through the main alignment of the body; the horse is therefore technically crooked; the joints of the hindlegs will be less inclined to flex, due to their sideways swinging action, slight though that may be.

Travers is therefore less directly conducive to collection than shoulder-in, and will not be used as a lead into other and more complicated movements as the latter is. Nevertheless it is a very useful exercise for loosening the upper joints of the hindlegs and for stretching the muscles of the quarters and loin in a lateral manner. The inside hindleg will not be able to take extra weight off the forehand as it will not come under the centre of gravity of the horse. The outside hindleg will however benefit in that respect. In both cases the effects of travers on the hindlegs are contrary to those produced by the shoulder-in in which the inside hindleg moves straight forward and under the centre of gravity, and has to flex in doing so.

So, for a travers-right:

a One or two half-halts to balance, alert and prepare both partners.

b Slide back the left or outside leg a hands breadth and apply a strong inward aid to move the quarters to the right, but only sufficiently to create the three tracks (see Fig. 18). The potential lateral flexibility of the horse is so limited that a four-track version of the travers would inevitably cause the shoulder-line to be at such acute an angle that the forelegs would have to cross too much and the impulsion, already inhibited by crookedness, would not carry forward through the poll and into the hand. The impulsion would also be inhibited by the presence of the wall when executed in a menage. But perhaps the major reason for not riding a travers on four tracks is that then neither hindleg would be working towards the centre of gravity.

c The rider's inside leg acts, simultaneously with the outside leg but well forward on the girth, to create and maintain the required bend and impulsion and to drive the forehand forward along the original track. As with shoulder-in, the inner leg may need to be supported at times in its forward-driving activity by some similar use of the outside leg which is, to that extent, dual purpose despite its position behind the girth.

d The inside hip and seat bone is pressed forward by a unilateral bracing of the loin which should result in a lengthening and sinking of the knee and heel to give maximum effectiveness of the aid. The rider must however continue to sit firmly on both seat bones.

e With the horse's head, neck and forehand moving, as they should, virtually straight ahead along the track, the hands and rein-aids have little part to play other than the frequent use of the fingers to make and release the half-halts and to keep the horse light on the inside rein.

f On completion of the travers, the rider must apply a lateral aid with his right or inside leg, drawn back behind the girth, to push the quarters outwards and back onto the track of the forelegs. Then both legs return to their normal positions on the girth to drive the horse forward on a single track, according to the gait.

The travers is usually employed only in trot. It may be used in walk as a preliminary introduction, but it is probably unwise to employ it very often in canter because of the risk of accentuating the horse's natural tendency to be crooked in that gait and the consequent ease which that can be turned into a bad habit.

Part 5 AIDS FOR RENVERS (on Three Tracks)

The aids for the renvers are, for all practical purposes, identical with the aids for travers. The only and relatively minor, difference between the two movements lies in the positioning of the hindlegs in relation to the main or original track.

In renvers, the hindquarters remain on the original track, the forelegs being taken onto a parallel but overlapping track.

In travers, as we have seen, the forelegs remain on the original track while the hindlegs are moved onto the parallel but overlapping track. (See Fig. 18 for differences and similarities.)

The renvers is a little more difficult to perform well than the travers because, when performed along the wall or boards of an arena, the

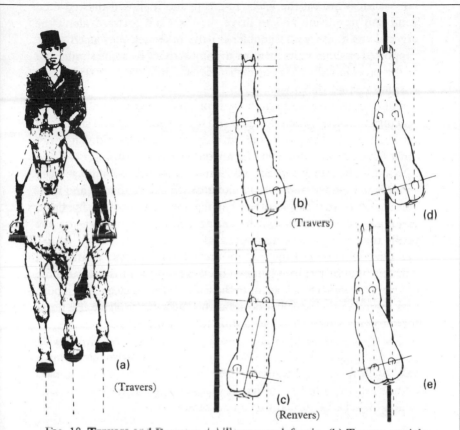

FIG 18 **Travers and Renvers.** (a) Travers on left rein. (b) Travers on right rein. (c) Renvers on right rein. (d) Travers-right on centre-line. (e) Renvers-right on centre-line.

horse does not have the close support of the wall to guide him and give him confidence.

Similarly, when performed along a marked centre-line (Fig. 18e), although there will be less difference in this case, again the horse will not have quite the same degree of confidence in his direction as he would have in travers because, in renvers, his head and eyes will not have a line to follow. He has to trust and obey the rider. The renvers therefore tends, in both instances, to require a more positive degree of riding.

Part 6 AIDS FOR HALF-PASS (Four Tracks) Fig. 17.5

Due to one of the several anomalies in the dressage language, the half-pass movement is often said to be 'on two tracks', and is sometimes even referred to by those words alone, especially by the French. That of course is satisfactory enough if it is compared only with the normal 'single' track progression of straight-forward riding. But if these matters are taken literally, the horse is always making two tracks in all straight-forward motion, one for his two right legs and a second parallel track for his two left legs. That incontrovertible fact of life is always disregarded and indeed never mentioned, though it would make much sense to give it full credit when thinking of all the multi-track and more or less lateral movements such as shoulder-in, travers and half-pass. There would then be a consistent logic in that, in every case, the number of tracks referred to would tally with those actually seen on sand or soft ground. If we follow that logic we would have to describe the half-pass as being a movement on four-tracks (Fig. 17e).

To summarise this logical method of describing lateral movements we should have the following situation:

On two tracks . . . all movement on straight lines, on large curves, and on circles down to the theoretical minimum of six-metre diameter.

On three tracks . . . shoulder-in, travers, renvers.

On four tracks . . . leg-yielding, half-pass, and pirouette.

N.B. There will be occasions during the process of adjusting the alignment of the horse from one of these movements to another, for example from straight-forward to shoulder-in, when the horse will for a moment be on four tracks between the original two and the ultimate three tracks. But these are temporary transitions and need not be considered in detail here.

The half-pass is the most difficult of all the lateral movements. In it the horse is required to move diagonally to one side while maintaining his original alignment, but bending and flexing in the direction of his movement, the front and back outside legs crossing over and in front of the inside legs. All four legs follow separate and parallel tracks (four tracks). It can be executed in all three gaits. The chief difficulty lies in the fact that the line of impulsion through the horse to the bit is not identical with the line of movement.

So, the aids for the right-half-pass will be:

a One or two half-halts to alert, balance and prepare both parties.

b Apply the aids for the right-shoulder-in (see Shoulder-in, page 72) and position the horse accordingly, because that is invariably the ideal position from which to start the half-pass. It ensures that the horse will, from the very beginning of the movement, have his forehand slightly in advance of his quarters, one of the prime requirements of this movement.

c Open the right hand by turning the thumb outwards, without changing the position of the forearm and, simultaneously, carry the left hand a little to the inside so that the line of the rein is directed towards the rider's right or inside hip. But the left hand must never cross the line of the neck. This left-rein action is to make use of the mechanical power of the fifth rein-effect (see Fig. 12e) to assist the whole movement to the right and to control the degree of bend in the neck.

d While sitting straight on both seat bones, put extra pressure into the left heel and use the left or outside leg predominantly and actively against the left side of the horse, as in leg-yielding and not too far back, to drive the whole horse onto his diagonal course to the right. If the horse has been properly trained up to this point and made sensitive to the leg-aids, it should not be necessary to turn the spur in towards the horse. Such an action, apart from being unsightly, and weakening the knee and thigh, is liable to have the disadvantage of making the horse too conscious of the sideways aspect of the half-pass at the expense of the equally important forwardness. It may also tend to push the quarters too rapidly to the side and so to make them lead the forehand which is always a fault. Should the horse be insufficiently responsive to the outside leg, it is better to assist it with light use of the whip on the same side and close behind the leg.

e The rider's inside leg remains active on the girth to maintain, along with the inside or right seat bone, the required bend through the fore-part of the horse's body and, at the same time, to maintain the impulsion forward and up to the bit. This latter aspect is the most difficult thing about the half-pass because, as we have already noted, of the difference between the lines of impulsion and actual movement. The solution requires acute awareness and sensitive coordination of the various aids of the seat, legs and hands.

N.B. Both legs have a combined and very important responsibility to keep the horse's hindlegs well engaged so that balance and collection are not lost, which is likely to happen if the impulsion is lost.

A useful idea to bear in mind is that it is at least theoretically possible to achieve a good half-pass by using the seat and legs solely for maintaining impulsion, and the hands and reins solely for controlling the direction and alignment of the horse (see Fig. 17). With this in mind it is clearly of vital importance that the hands and reins do not cross each other, as is often seen, and so be working in direct mutual contradiction.

Part 7 AIDS FOR PIROUETTES

A pirouette, or half-pirouette, is nothing more than a half-pass on a very small circle or half-circle. It can be executed in walk and in canter, but in trot-form only in piaffe.

Since all pirouettes are performed almost on the spot, they require the highest degree of collection in order to maintain the correct sequence and rhythm of the gait. This, in canter, puts considerable strain on the quarters which have to flex strongly and engage deeply in order to carry the major proportion of the overall weight. Excessive use of the exercise should be avoided. If the horse is frightened of the strain he will never perform it well.

In the walk, and also in the piaffe/trot, the pivot of the turn will be the inside hindleg which should move around a circle the size of a saucer.

In canter, the pivot of the turn will be the outside hindleg because, in the peculiar and asymmetrical sequence of that gait, the outside hindleg is the only leg available and capable of pushing the horse to the side in each of the separate though connected segments of the complete (360 degrees) or semi (180 degrees) circle. In addition, no turning movement is possible while the second-beat diagonal, which includes the inside hindfoot, is on the ground. In canter the outside hindleg should move around a circle the size of a dinner plate.

Although the rhythm and sequence of the canter should ideally remain unbroken and the same before, during and when coming out of the pirouette, in practice a slight break in the diagonal or second beat of the canter is usually tolerated because of the extreme difficulty of maintaining the pure diagonal in the maximum and shortened collection that is required in which the horse is more or less 'sitting' on his haunches. And in that connection, it is of great importance that the horse should not flatten his back and then clearly lift his forehand round inactive and grounded hindlegs. The latter must remain active in true canter form, with a clear distinction between the two footfalls and with the inner leg stepping well forward and under the weight, towards the centre of gravity, from which position alone the horse can control his whole body in one piece in this most difficult movement.

When the hindlegs fail to act firmly and separately, the horse will appear to perform his part in two pieces, comprising a small hop with the two hindlegs nearly in unison, followed by a lifted-swing with the forehand. It will bear no resemblance to a true canter.

Throughout the whole pirouette, which should comprise between six and eight steps in canter, the horse should remain very light, consistently on the bit and flexed in the direction of the turn.

Unless and until a horse can perform a very collected canter, almost on the spot, for the few strides, he cannot be expected to perform a satisfactory pirouette.

Part 8 AIDS FOR WALK-PIROUETTE, RIGHT

a Collect the walk, which must be very active and very collected and with no slowing of the tempo, by a series of half-halts.

b When the hindfeet reach the appointed spot on which the pirouette or half-pirouette has to be performed, apply a stronger half-halt with the outside rein accompanied by stronger activating leg-aids to ensure the continued activity and engagement of the hindlegs, even as the forward movement virtually ceases. The horse must continue to be driven up to the hand.

c The rider's left or outside leg moves well back behind the girth, the heel well down to ensure that the weight remains firm on that seat bone, acting as a guard against any tendency of the quarters to deviate to the left or get the horse to turn on its centre, but still taking an active part in maintaining the forward impulsion.

d The right or inside leg remains active in a forward manner on the girth to encourage the bend and flexion to the right. The legs should now alternate as the hindleg on each side lifts from the ground or is in the air (see Chapter 2 Part 2 page 42).

e The right or inside hand opens slightly to lead the forehand round and into the first steps of the pirouette. However, if the inside leg is doing its work effectively, it is the outside rein that dominates and controls the size and speed of the turn, the inside rein retaining only a light contact.

f The rider sits square with his pelvis, but turns his shoulders a little to the right in the direction of the pirouette, in accordance with the horse's bend. The rider looks above the horse's ears.

g The combined aids take the horse, step by step, round the pirouette, the seat and legs being active throughout to ensure that there is no break in the footfall sequence during the turn or during the eventual transition into the forward walk or other movement that will follow.

Aids for Piaffe-Pirouette

The aids will be precisely as for the walk with the exception that, the movement being in trot-rhythm, the leg-aids will act together instead of alternately (see also Piaffe, page 92).

Aids for Canter-Pirouette

The pirouette in canter is much more difficult than it is in either walk or piaffe, due to the necessity for the horse in this gait to keep up the more complicated rhythm which includes a moment of suspension and in which the number of feet-on-the-ground to support his weight will vary in the sequence 1,3,2,3,1,0 (see Fig. 15 page 62). To achieve that correct sequence he has to spring into the air for the moment of complete suspension at the end of each stride without moving significantly forward. This is a considerable gymnastic feat and in practice the suspension is very seldom achieved.

The aids will be:

a A series of half-halts to shorten and collect the canter until it is making very little forward progress and with the horse carrying a high proportion of his weight on his lowered and well-engaged haunches.

b Before beginning the actual pirouette, and while still on the original alignment, place the horse in a slight shoulder-in position, bearing in mind that the pirouette is only a half-pass on a small circle and that the shoulder-in is the ideal posture from which to start a half-pass, and therefore also a pirouette. Failure to do this will result in a tendency for the pirouette to start with the quarters leading which, in turn, will make it extremely difficult for the horse to take his forehand around them, as the quarters keep getting in the way. As in all half-passes, the forehand must be slightly in advance of the quarters throughout the movement.

c With a series of strong canter-half-halts, originating from a powerfully braced loin and with a well lowered right or inside leg on the girth, the rider leads the horse, canter-step by canter-step, round the pirouette (or half-pirouette), with a light inside rein supported and controlled by the outside rein. The inside rein leads, but must not pull the horse round.

d The half-pass effect must be maintained by the domination control of the left or outside seat bone and leg, the heel of the latter pressed well down towards the ground.

e Notwithstanding the dominating effect of the outside lateral aids, the inside leg has a vital role to play in controlling the speed of the turn; in maintaining the bend and so preventing the horse from throwing himself round on his shoulder; and in enforcing obedience by demanding that the horse waits on the permission of the inside leg before making the next step round the circle. He must be trained to have the patience to move only stride by stride, as permitted. Only when that obedience is present will the rider be in true control of his horse and able to ride forwards and out of the pirouette at any point he may select.

f Throughout the six to eight steps of a full pirouette, or three to four in a half-pirouette, the hands must be quiet and must never try to pull the horse round, any more than they try to pull the horse to the side in half-pass. The action must be achieved by the correct coordination of all the aids as it was in the half-pass, the seat and legs being predominant; the horse playing a willing part, without coming off the bit and without hollowing the back; and the rhythm and tempo remaining the same as they were before the turn began.

g In order to keep the horse in front of him, and so remain in control, the rider must retain his firm seat by pressing his pelvis forward and his stomach into the hands, so that the pelvis will always be leading the torso and the forward impulsion be maintained.

CHAPTER SIX

Aids for Special Movements

Part 1 AIDS FOR REIN-BACK AND SCHAUKEL

In the rein-back the horse steps back in two-time, or almost two-time, sequence. The former must be regarded as ideal. In the schaukel, (German; see-saw) the horse steps back a prescribed number of steps and then, without halting or becoming immobile, is ridden forward in walk for another prescribed number of steps to be followed, again without halting or immobility, by a second rein-back. The last rein-back is followed, without immobility, by a move forward directly into any of the three gaits. Each foot should be picked cleanly off the ground; not dragged along; and returned cleanly and precisely to the ground.

Each 'leg' of the schaukel or the rein-back has to be ridden in smooth, unresistant and regular rhythm, the horse remaining on the bit, and without dragging his feet. He must never be, or appear to be, pulled backwards by the reins, each rearward step being the result of being ridden forward into restraining hands.

The Aids
After being brought into a square halt by the normal aids described in Chapter 4, and standing on the bit and on the aids:

a The rider braces his back and closes both legs on the girth to press the horse forward, as if for walk-on. While doing this he may lean almost imperceptibly forward to take a little of his weight off his seat bones to free the horse's back-muscles which are under considerable strain in this slightly unnatural movement.

b Just as, *but not before*, he feels the horse to be lifting a foot or beginning to sway forward into walk, the rider firmly closes both hands to oppose the forward movement, but taking strict care not to move the elbows back . . . not to pull back. The hands must remain absolutely still, apart from the closing of the fingers. Nor must the shoulders lean back.

This action of the hands and reins will result in the already-felt impulsion being rechannelled to the rear so that the horse will step quietly backwards instead of forwards, in diagonal steps without resistance to the rein in mouth, poll, neck or back.

c As the horse responds by stepping back, the leg-aids are somewhat relaxed but remain in contact to maintain a modicum of the forward impulsion into the bit, even though the horse is actually moving back. The rein contact is also maintained with the fingers closed in opposition, *and must not exert any backward pull.*

d As the rider feels the last of the required number of backward steps being taken, and before the foot is grounded, he firmly reasserts the forward influence of his seat and legs to cause the horse to move into the forward walk again without pausing on that last backward step. The foot may ground, but should not become weighted, as that would cause a degree of immobility and spoil the fluency of the movement.

e As the renewed leg-aid is applied, the fingers open on the reins sufficiently to allow the horse to walk forward without loss of contact.

f When a full schaukel is being performed, as opposed to a single rein-back-and-forward, the rider again applies the aids already described for the rein-back, this time just before he feels the horse is about to ground the foot that is taking the last of the required steps forward.

N.B. 1. Steps to the rear are counted as each diagonal pair grounds. Steps to the front are counted by the alternate forelegs.

N.B. 2. If the rider commits the sin of pulling back with the reins, even if ever so little, there will be a tendency for the horse to resist the aid by stiffening in the mouth, poll or back. That resistance will find its way through to the joints of the hindlegs. The rein-back will then become more or less jerky, as if under protest, with broken rhythm in the footfalls, and possibly crooked or with spreading hindlegs. The

FIG 19 **Rein-Back with incorrect leg position**, not on girth and heel raised. Rider unable to retain impulsion.

feet may drag along the ground instead of being cleanly picked up and precisely replaced on the ground. All these things are bad faults and are almost invariably the result of incorrect aids and some degree of pulling.

N.B. 3. It is quite unnecessary, and is an obvious weakness, for the rider to make the rein-back with his legs held back against the horse's flanks, presumably for the purpose of trying to keep the horse straight. Since the legs cannot, from that rear position, push the horse forward into the hand with impulsion, as has been described above as essential to the efficiency of the movement, this fault is usually accompanied and compounded by a pulling-back on the reins and a complete loss of impulsion, the horse probably lengthening himself and poking his nose. It is sadly a fault that is very commonly seen at all levels.

Part 2 AIDS FOR FLYING CHANGES OF LEG (Canter)

When a horse that is cantering on the right lead makes a flying-change-of-leg to canter on the left lead, he does so by making a complete change in the footfall-sequence but without any loss or break in the canter rhythm. This adjustment of his footfall-sequence is only possible during the brief moment when, after the completion of a full canter-stride, all four feet will be off the ground and in suspension. Only then are they free to be adjusted. But if that adjustment is made correctly and fluently, the continuity of the rhythm will be such that a blind man would not be able to tell that a change had been made.

There is nothing intrinsically different about a flying-change, either for the horse or for the rider. In practice, however, there are problems for both parties in the early stages and until practice makes perfect.

Every horse can and will make perfectly correct flying-changes while cantering loose around a field, and from his earliest youth. But he makes those virtuoso changes by the light of nature, without thinking about how he does it, and probably without being conscious of doing it. The problems arise when he is asked to think a little in order to make a change of leg precisely and only when asked to by his rider and by means of a not very intelligible language.

For the rider, the problems are relatively small, provided only that he has thoroughly mastered and understood the aids for the strike-off into canter from the halt, and also from the walk and the trot, as already described in Chapter 4, Part 3. If he and his horse can make a clear-cut strike-off, or canter-depart, from the halt into either lead, it becomes only a matter of timing to achieve a canter-depart into the right-lead from an existing canter-left. But the timing and the clarity of the aids for the new canter-depart become crucial, just because the moment of suspension, without which the action is not predictable, is so brief.

It has become conventional to speak of a cantering horse as leading with his left, or with his right, foreleg. That is of course perfectly valid and is quite readily seen. But in fact the horse, when in a true canter, will always be leading with both the foreleg and the hindleg on the same side. But it is the hindlegs that dictate the lead. When considering flying-changes however, it is of greater importance to remember that each and every canter stride, of whichever lead, always begins with, and has its source in, the hindleg on the side opposite to the lead. The canter-left originates in the right hindleg; the canter-right in the left hindleg. It is that originating leg that should have first claim to the attention of the rider. That is the leg that has to initiate the new footfall sequence. That is the leg that has to answer first to the rider's aids. If that new initiating or outside leg has responded correctly and fluently to the rider's seat-and-leg aid, a correct and complete flying-change will almost invariably follow.

If the rider thinks only about the foreleg, he will probably fail. If he concentrates on the new outside hindleg, he will probably succeed and achieve a good flying-change.

We will consider precisely what the rider expects from the horse's hindlegs when he asks for a flying-change. We are going to change from canter-right to canter-left.

a The existing canter-right is being initiated by the left hindleg.

b The new canter-left must be initiated by the right hindleg. Otherwise it cannot happen.

c The right hindleg has hitherto been grounding as the second beat of the existing canter-right, and after the left hindleg. But it must now, suddenly though smoothly and during the brief moment of suspension, come forward more quickly so as to pass the left hindleg in the air; to come to the ground before it; and become the first beat of the canter instead of the second.

d The left hindleg will now, having had its initiating role usurped by the right one, become part of the second or diagonal beat of the new canter-left.

The action of the horse's hindlegs is identical to that of the legs of a small child who, holding its mother's hand, skips along the pavement, putting down each leg twice in quick succession. That action will be right-right, left-left, right-right, etc. And when flying-changes are made in one-time sequence, or every stride, the hindleg action continues to be identical to that of the child. The hindlegs dictate the rhythm. The forelegs comply and follow-on.

So, since the flying-changes is no more than a new strike-off in motion, the aids for flying-changes are, to all practical purposes, the same as those for the simple strike-off, to right or to left. They say the same things for the same purpose, although there are some slight differences in timing and expression.

1 The rider cannot take his time. He is the servant of that brief moment of total suspension. He must do his job within those unforgiving restrictions, and also make some allowance for the message to get through the horse's mental and nervous system in good time.

2 For the simple strike-off, the rider had to create impulsion from zero. Now, for the flying-change and with the horse already in motion, he has not so much to create but to maintain impulsion throughout a quite difficult proceedure in which there is an inherent tendency.

The Aids for the Flying-change (canter right to canter left)

It is now time to summarise the aids for the flying-change, for the strike-off in the air, remembering all the good habits we have acquired for dealing with the simpler forms of strike-off. In particular it must be remembered that we need to use *all* our active aids, that is to say the weight, the loins, the seat bones and both legs. The latter point is as valid for the flying-changes as it is for all other demands we may make on the horse.

a The timing will differ very slightly with different horses and riders, but it is generally best to try to begin the aid-sequence on the second beat of the canter stride. It will then be completed by the end of the third beat (Fig. 15.5), by which time both the hindlegs will be off the ground and free to begin the change of sequence. By the moment of full suspension (Fig. 15.6) the change must be actually taking place, and so it will be seen that the rider cannot afford to be late with that first move at or about the second beat (Fig. 15.2 or 3).

b Brace the right loin to depress the right seat bone, knee and heel, the leg sliding a little to the rear of its previous position on the girth. This aid does two things. The seat bone indicates to the horse that he should bring his right hindleg into action to carry the extra weight, and the sliding back of the leg indicates that it will no longer be demanding another canter-right stride.

c Brace the left loin strongly and thrust forward the left hip and seat bone in conjunction with a lowering of the left heel and a strong left leg-aid applied on the girth. This aid also does two things. It tends to put the horse into the correct position for canter-left with its slight bend round the rider's new inside leg, and it simultaneously demands increased activity from the left fore and hind legs to encourage them to adopt their new leading role.

d Close both legs in their new positions (the positions for canter-left), brace the loins; drive the seat bones forward (to lead the torso) to push the horse forward with impulsion into the new and complete canter-stride.

N.B. Throughout these almost, but not quite, simultaneous actions the rider should ensure that his legs never lose their contact with the horse, as far down to the ankle as possible; that his seat bones remain firmly in the saddle, with a tendency to lead the torso; and that, despite his activities and concentration on timing, he remains relaxed and supple from head to heel, so that he can feel and follow the horse's movement. All the aids must be independent of each other, and any stiffening of the loin or torso will make that impossible.

The rider must try to feel as if he were part of his horse; to move in harmony with it; and to make the change as if he were changing his own legs, the horse following like a good dancing partner.

Part 2(B) AIDS FOR SEQUENCE CHANGES OF LEG

The aids for continuous sequence flying-changes, that is to say changes performed in regular sequence every six, five, four, three, two, or even every (one) stride, are exactly the same as those for the occasional or single flying-changes. But the fact remains however that the greater the number of strides that occur between successive changes of leg, the easier it is for the horse and for the rider to regain any loss of balance or impulsion that may have been lost during the last change of leg. It follows that changes performed every two strides (two-time changes) or every stride (one-time changes) require a very high degree of balance from the horse and of aid-finesse from the rider. One-time changes in particular are widely regarded as one of the pinnacles of artistic equestrian achievement, at any rate when ridden well without noticeable movement or effort from the rider.

Changes down to two-time, or every second stride, do not require additional or special comment, since horse and rider have at least one clear and normal stride after each change of leg in which to readjust themselves or to cope with any little problem that may have arisen such as crookedness or loss of impulsion or engagement. In the latter context it is always important to ensure that the hindlegs do remain well engaged during each change of leg. If they tend to get left behind, the horse will not have the power from his back to remain in balance and the change will not go through-and-forward. This problem is a prime concern of the rider's seat-and-legs which should remain in contact, sensitive and active at all times. It is also a prime reason for insisting that the seat and pelvis remain in the saddle, leading the torso, so that the rider is never in front of the movement from which position he could not influence impulsion.

Changes in one-time, with the change executed with absolute regularity at the end of every stride, are a rather special case as they permit of no time for anything but the finest of adjustments that the rider may feel arising in the course of the sequence of perhaps ten or fifteen or twenty changes. If they are to be done well and with credit to the rider and trainer, the rider's aids and the horse's responses must have been exquisitely refined in quality and in timing. Nothing should be seen except a horse changing his legs at every step like the child skipping down the street. This is the movement, above all others, in which the horse should 'appear to be doing of his own accord what is required of him'.

But be that as it may, many quite famous riders will be seen resorting to all sorts of excessive movements of their bodies and legs when riding one-time, and sometimes even two-time, changes. Their seat leaves the saddle; their torso gets in front of their pelvis; and their legs swing widely like a windscreen-wiper on a car. These and similar faults are not a credit to them and should not be copied by other riders with ambition. At best they are highly unaesthetic to look at, and at worst they are disturbing and unfair to the horse that is expected to be much better in control of himself.

We have already noted that, due to the extremely limited time factor in one-time changes, the rider has to develop and use highly refined aids. Changes are made in all cases by appropriate use of seat and leg aids, those two aspects being in practice inextricably linked. All leg-aids have their source in the seat, and it follows that the more refined they become the more the seat takes over from the legs. That does not mean that the legs should ever be discarded. They must remain in contact in their appropriate positions where they are ready in an instant to be called into action to take an increased part in the proceedings, if necessary, and from where they can always maintain or increase impulsion.

It is nevertheless a fact that, provided at least that the legs remain in contact, the aids of the weight and seat bones are all that are required to create good one-time or other short-sequence flying-changes. In general practice, complete immobility of the legs is not essential, and it is helpful if they play their part in the totality of the aids. They will continue to press a little at the appropriate moment. Perhaps they will move an inch to the rear or front, moving as it were only within a stationary boot so that the spectator will notice nothing. They will move and breath in harmony with the swing of the horse from one lead to the other. But it should, with every excellent rider, be the pelvis and seat bones that talk the loudest. The legs should only whisper in harmony.

The key to the good riding of one-time changes lies in the supple and active use of the small of the back, the loin, acting to push the pelvis forward over the seat bones, in conjunction with the looseness of the knee and the lowering of the heel.

Part 3 AIDS FOR PIAFFE

The aids for the piaffe are similar to those for the Trot-On (Chapter 2, Part 2), but with the following distinctions:

a The rider's legs are taken a little back behind their normal position on the girth, but act simultaneously, with heels sunk.

1 To indicate to the horse that he is not being required to move forward very much; in other words a distinction that he will understand.

2 To indicate that the rider's legs are speaking directly to the horse's hindlegs which must respond promptly and energetically.

b The rider's loin is braced more strongly than usual but essentially with spring-like resiliance, to encourage the horse's back to swing and remain round. The rider's supple loin must make allowance for the increased upward motion that is inherent in this trot-on-the-spot.

c The reins act only as strongly as may be necessary to restrain the forward movement. The aim should be to make the piaffe with the lightest possible contact with the horse's mouth so that the horse feels the bit but is in no way restricted by it during the hightly gymnastic requirements of the piaffe that should be performed with much cadence and elevation, especially of the forehand.

If the quarters are sufficiently engaged and lowered, though not excessively engaged as when the hindfeet come in front of the vertical line through the stifle, the forehand will automatically become very light and a strong contact with the bit will be superfluous.

d Throughout, the rider must sit very still so as not to disturb the horse's balance and concentration, using virtually invisible aids through his loins and lengthened legs. The use of the spur, apart from the occasional and helpful touch, is to be avoided as it is unsightly, spoils the rider's seat, and often results in resistance and even kicking. The rider should not appear to be doing the work instead of the horse.

Part 4 AIDS FOR PASSAGE

The passage gait is, in essence, very similar to the piaffe except for the fact that the horse must thrust himself forward as well as upward in order to make limited progress to the front. Though very collected his body will, as in trot, remain nearly horizontal instead of 'sitting' as in piaffe.

The aids for passage are similar to those of piaffe, but with the following distinctions:

a Since the horse must continue to make substantial, if limited, forward progress, the rider's legs should remain in their normal position on the girth to create maximum impulsion and engagement of the hindlegs.

b The same strong but resilient bracing of the loin is required to initiate the passage, but the accompanying leg-aids should be of a more than usually lengthened and 'wrap-round' nature with much squeeze. They should be held-on for a somewhat longer period to compensate for the prolonged period of suspension inherent in this gait, acting in an alternating aid-release-aid-release rhythm in time with the steps. This differs from the ordinary trot for which the leg-aids are more vibrant or even tapping, and generally quicker. This prolonged holding-on of the leg-aid serves several purposes:

1 It is an indication to the horse that a somewhat different form of trot is demanded.

2 It helps to differentiate between the passage and the piaffe in which the legs were held back in a distinctly different position and acted vibrantly, simultaneously, but also in rhythm.

3 It allows for the slower but strongly cadenced rhythm of the horse as he lifts himself into the prolonged suspension between the alternate diagonals. It also encourages that extra lift and suspension.

N.B. 1. As with the piaffe, the rider must sit very still, with the lightest possible contact with the reins, thus allowing the maximum freedom of the horse through his whole structure.

N.B. 2. It is vital that, before anyone attempts to teach a young horse the passage, the rider should have acquired a strong, firm seat with a supple and fully controlled back so that he will be able to sit through the powerful upward thrusts of the passage gait. If he cannot sit well, his bumping seat will act as a positive discouragement to his horse.

Part 5 THE GALLOP FOOTFALL

The conventional lore of dressage recognises the three gaits of walk, trot and canter. But there is also a fourth perfectly natural gait, the gallop, that never gets mentioned or studied. This omission is the more strange in that the fifth century Greek Xenophon, the undisputed Father of Dressage, trained his horses primarly for war and much of their work was certainly done at the full gallop.

The footfall-sequence of the gallop is quite different and distinct from that of the canter (see Fig. 20) and must therefore be acknowledged as a gait in its own right. It is unfortunate and a little confusing that the French and the Germans use the same word for the three-beat canter, the gallop being essentially a four-beat gait.

The distinctive feature of the real gallop is that the horse becomes stretched to his limit with each step and stride and also that the period of suspension after each full stride is greatly prolonged.

The canter has five distinct phases, in five of which either one, two or three feet are grounded.

1		2		3		4		5		6		7
♩		♩			♩		♩		♩			prolonged suspension
	♩		♩						♩		♩	

FIG 20 **The Gallop Footfalls.** Compare with fig. 15.
Note seven phases, in six of which either one or two, but never three feet
are grounded. All steps, and also the period of suspension, are greatly
lengthened.

The gallop has seven distinct phases, in six of which either one or
two, but never three, feet are grounded. The balance and stability of
the canter is consequently much more secure than in the gallop.

When running loose in a field, horses will frequently adopt the
gallop out of sheer exuberance and to give expression to their sense of
fun and well-being. But because of the problems of balance already
mentioned in connection with never having more than two feet on the
ground at once, they cannot switch into gallop until a certain
minimum speed has been attained. It is difficult to balance a bicycle
until it is moving reasonably fast. To overcome this problem, the
horse in the field can be seen, when moving off in a hurry from
perhaps a halt or a walk, to get up speed quickly by means of perhaps
ten or more very quick, short, powerful canter strides. Only then will
he suddenly change gear into the fully stretched but comparatively
slow tempo gallop in which, among other things, he covers many
metres of ground while he is in full suspension.

In contemporary mounted activities, the gallop is regularly used in
cattle ranching, hunting, polo and, above all else, in racing.

It cannot be said that there are any specific aids for the gallop,
though in modern times most riders and jockeys assist the horse and
add to their own comfort by adopting a posture in which their whole
weight is balanced over their knees and stirrups and not at all on their
seat which probably has no contact with the saddle. However, it was
not always thus, and well into the twentieth century professional
jockeys, on the flat and over fences, were riding their races and even
their finishes, in an upright posture and using their seat and loins as
an aid to improve their horse's speed. Moreover, it is by no means
certain that the more recent adoption of the forward-balanced posture
that is now regarded as the standard racing 'seat', originating from
the American jockey Tod Sloane, has as much effect on the
racehorse's speed as we are tempted to assume.

As a test of the effectiveness of the forward-seat on racing speeds, we can examine the timings of the winners of the Grand National steeplechase at Aintree, over a distance of approximately four and a half miles. In the early days, when the course was virtually all fairly heavy plough and without rails and with some very curious fences, including a rough stone wall, the winner's time varied, according to the state of the going and the weather, and to certain other changes that were made from time to time, between ten and thirteen minutes. Between 1845 and 1885 it was almost always won in well under eleven minutes.

In 1885, the course became all grass for the first time and was fully railed on the inside. In the thirty years from then until the first world war, during which the National was not run, the times settled down to between nine-and-a-half and ten-and-a-half minutes.

In 1947, all the fences were strongly sloped on the take-off side to make jumping safer, easier and, presumably, faster. But from then on, for the last forty years, and although the ten-minute times have almost disappeared, the average has remained obstinately higher than nine-and-a-half minutes.

The lesson to be learnt from the point of view of the riding methods concerns the fact that right into the 'thirties, and even up to the last war, it was considered essential for all the jockeys to sit and lean right back over the jumps, with their legs stuck out in front of them to take the strain, as the only practical means of surviving the rigours of those famous fences. The Caprilli and McTaggart theories of the forward-seat were beginning to be accepted as reasonable for enthusiastic amateurs in the hunting field and the show-ring, but were ruled out as ludicrously inappropriate for steeplechasing. The pace made it impossible, it was said.

So it was not until the 'fifties, when a break was made with many an old tradition and one or two great jockeys began to show the way, that we saw the beginnings of the present day brilliant phase of jump-jockeyship. Now, as the television and the newspapers show it is extraordinarily rare to see those brave riders out of place or being dragged over the fences by their horse's mouths. They are without doubt, and as a group, the best stylists and exponents of good horsemanship in any of the many forms of modern equestrian activity. And yet, we have to admit, the winning times of the National have not dropped accordingly. The Winters, the Francomes the

O'Neills and the Turnells have not been getting round Aintree any faster than their ancestors, and we can only assume that we moderns don't know it all. The old 'uns certainly sat on their seat more, but perhaps they knew a thing or two about using them that we have missed out on or forgotten. In that context it is almost certainly relevant that, at any rate until a very few years ago, the French National and ex-Cavalry School at Saumur insisted that their students mastered the art of jumping fences fast, sitting bolt upright and without reins, before they were allowed to discover the pleasures of swinging forward over the knees. And they did not lean or fall off backwards, either. It was possible and they did it, and in doing so they learnt how to use their loins to 'go-along' with their horses. We have heard that phrase earlier on in this book. It doubtless applied to the best of the steeplechase jockeys and foxhunting men of the last century.

CHAPTER SEVEN

Exercises for the Rider

W E ALL KNOW that dressage horses, like all other athletes, have to be supple. We all know that no athlete or horse is ever sufficiently supple if left to his own devices, and that the dressage rider's first priority is to make and to keep his horse supple throughout its body and limbs. Without suppleness, the horse is a dreary and uncomfortable thing to ride. It can never aspire to gymnastic excellence.

A glance at the last lines of the Preface to this book will remind us that the first of the three mottoes recommended for aspiring dressage riders stated that 'no horse can be better than its rider'. No horse develops its dressage education of its own free will. Being a relatively unintelligent animal, it has to be educated by its human trainer, the limits of that education being set by the limits of the trainer's various abilities. It follows that only a supple rider can make a supple horse. Further, and perhaps worse, an unsupple rider, or one who has through negligence allowed himself to become stiff, will quite quickly destroy any suppleness that a horse may already have acquired and will make dressage progress impossible.

In short, a horse ridden by a stiff and therefore insensitive rider will become stiff and insensitive itself, through the insensitivity of the treatment it will have received.

Clearly it behoves every would-be dressage rider to check on his own fitness for the job before he begins to concern himself about his horse. He needs knowledge and understanding about what he is intending to do, and he needs physical fitness and suppleness to enable him to carry it out.

Sadly it must be admitted that too few people give these matters sufficient thought. They assume that they will acquire a modicum of knowledge as they go along, making endless mistakes at the expense of the unfortunate horse. And they mostly assume that, because they are able to run to catch a bus, they can claim to be supple. Or maybe they have been hacking or hunting for many years, and so surely they are supple enough. But quite definitely that is invariably untrue. Suppleness has to be fought for, not hoped for.

Every experienced and successful dressage rider knows that the suppleness of his horse is something that has to be worked on every single day, even to maintain its existing standard. And so it is with human beings. Perhaps children in their teens are truly and beautifully supple, but all adults past the age of twenty become progressively stiffer unless they take the trouble to take very positive steps to regain or improve their suppleness.

Just riding regularly, though it may well help to keep the doctor away, is not enough, in fact it is almost useless for our purpose. We can be stiff and awkward on our feet all our lives, and so we can on horseback. But it is quite unnecessary for us to be like that, though the problem has to be treated seriously and regularly. Take for example the great ballet dancers of the world. They have had to fight for that position by striving continuously for greater fitness, strength and suppleness. From their early childhood to the end of their dancing careers they work every single day 'at the bar', stretching, suppling and strengthening all parts of themselves with routine, strenuous and often painful exercises.

The rider's problems are admittedly less demanding, but they certainly exist and need to be tackled in a manner similar to that used by the dancers if the combined progress and ultimate performance of horse and-rider is not to suffer.

The conscientious dressage rider's target should be a fit and supple body, fit and above all supple from his head to his heels. And that, in all seriousness, is a lifetime task. It is not just a question of doing a little jogging, combined with a few deep-breathing exercises each morning. It involves, in the fullest sense, an extensive examination of every muscle, sinew and joint in the body, though that may be more than the average rider is willing or able to cope with. But to find out what is possible, and to get some idea of his own current shortcomings or disabilities, each rider would profit from taking a comparatively short and investigatory course under a teacher of Yoga or of the Alexander System. He would then be able to work out some shortened daily work-programme suited to his individual physique and life-style. Such a programme might require anything from three to fifteen minutes each morning, or at any other time of the day that might be convenient. Three minutes would be better than nothing and could work wonders. No one could say that they do not have the time for that.

Such exercises are done of course indoors, in the warm, and in a relaxed atmosphere where there are no interruptions. They have to be done, however few of them, in conditions where the person can concentrate entirely and unhurriedly on his own body. The conventional riding-school exercises performed from the saddle, such as swinging the arms, touching the toes, or twisting the body, are of comparatively little use and rather bad luck on the long-suffering horse. The rider should, with humility, put himself right for the day before he climbs stiffly onto his horse. Only then is he justified in beginning to work on the horse. He must remember that the muscles of the horse's back will suffer immediately and considerably if the rider cannot or does not sit correctly and supply in the saddle. And everytime the horse is subjected to such suffering or inconvenience, the clock of the training programme will be put back. It is a false assumption that the horse will quickly recover, forgive and forget.

This is no place to begin writing a treatise on the basic principles of Yoga or the Alexander System, or even to outline the many hundreds of exercises comprised in those systems. Nevertheless a few notes may help to indicate how the matter might be approached and to outline some of the potential benefits to a rider.

1 Suppleness concerns ligaments and muscles.

2 Muscles are capable of contracting or stretching.

3 Muscles tend to contract when at rest or in sleep.

4 Every muscle must be stretched before it can be made supple. When the dog or cat gets out of bed, it first stretches its limbs. Otherwise it will not be supple enough to catch the rabbit or the mouse.

5 The rider must become supple every day to enable him to ride his horse efficiently and without doing harm.

6 The horse must also be first stretched and then made supple every day before he can be expected to move freely in a gymnastic manner and to respond easily and smoothly to the rider's demands.

7 The stretching, suppling and strengthening of a dressage horse is

a long and progressive business which, if properly carried out, will make a visible improvement in the horses's musculature and general physique, rendering him capable of executing with ease the most difficult and strenuous exercises and movements.

8 The areas of muscle in the rider's body that require particular attention if he is to ride correctly and easily are the following:

a *The loin and small of the back*, which must be capable of holding the pelvis in a more or less vertical posture to convey the weight of the torso directly onto the seat bones. The loin muscles must be loose and supple enough to swing the pelvis forward so that it 'goes along' with the movement of the horse and leads the torso forward.

b *The front of the thigh*, where the muscles must be stretched and free enough to allow the leg to hang down without constraint; for the knee to drop when required; and for the pelvis to be able to ride forward over the knee as it swings with the movement of the horse.

c *The back of the thigh*, to give strength to the leg-aids that flow from the seat into the lowered heel.

d *The shoulders*, to allow them to be carried flat and low, with the chest open and not cramped so that it interferes with the uprightness of the torso as a whole or with the swing of the pelvis underneath it.

e *The neck*, so that it can be carried erect and still, so that the considerable weight of the head will not disturb the overall balance of the torso.

Those five areas of muscle, areas in which stiffness can spoil everything and suppleness can bring success, are admittedly only the most important of many. But if the rider keeps those five in good condition, he will not be going too far wrong. He will at least feel that he is trying, for the benefit of himself and his horse.

SUGGESTED MINIMAL EXERCISES

Serious instruction and advice from a trained teacher is of course desirable, but in default of that the following minimal sequence of exercises, requiring from three to five minutes, may give an idea of what the author has in mind.

101

1 Take five or six deep breaths, followed in each case with the deepest possible exhalation in an effort to empty the lungs of all stale air.

2 Stand in front of and at right-angles to a mirror. With the head upright, turn it slowly three times to the right, making sure that the chin points directly over the shoulder, towards the mirror. Turn round and repeat the process to the other side. The purpose – to release restrictions in the neck muscles.

3 Lie face down on the floor, with the feet in the air, and take hold of the insteps with the hands. Slowly pull the chest and the knees off the ground. Hold the position for ten seconds. Repeat three times.

It may be advisable to begin, for the first day or so, to pull up the chest only; then the knees only; and finally both at once. The knees should rise three or four inches from the floor. The purpose – to stretch the muscles at the front of the thighs, the small of the back, and the shoulders. Those are the vital muscles that allow the rider to sit upright and supply.

4 Kneel up, with knees about one foot apart. Then lean slowly back to place the hands on the soles of the feet, keeping the pelvis up and forward. Hold the position for ten seconds, breathing freely. Repeat three times.

5 Stand up, with feet one foot apart and toes to the front. With the hands on the small of the back, lean backwards as far as possible, pushing the pelvis, forward, the head well back and breathing freely. Hold the position for ten seconds. Repeat three times. The purpose – the chest and the breathing. Relax and have breakfast.

CHAPTER EIGHT

Exercises for the Horse

IN THE PREVIOUS chapter we looked at some of the problems connected with the need for physical exercises that help to make the rider fit, or at any rate fitter, for his job of training a dressage horse. We did not attempt to discuss the aims and objectives of dressage training in general or in detail. We spoke only of the essential personal preparations that each rider should make, and without which he would be in grave danger of failing in his task.

In this chapter, and on the assumption that we start with a reasonably well prepared rider, we shall look at the same problem of preparation as it affects the horse. We shall not discuss any of the normally accepted dressage movements such as the shoulder-in, half-pass or the flying-change, but only the physical qualities and states to be achieved before those movements are attempted, or at least before they can be efficiently accomplished.

The exercises for the horse fall into three logically successive phases, those of Loosening, Stretching, Suppling. All three phases, in that order, should be worked on every day as an essential preliminary to the serious and progressive work of improving old lessons and teaching new ones. To try to work on the old or the new lessons without running through these preliminary exercises is illogical, unintelligent and unsympathetic. No human being or animal is at his best immediately he steps out of bed. No dancer can attempt to perform his more difficult routines until he has spent a little time 'on the bar' to loosen, stretch and supple his muscles. No concert pianist will attempt to play a major piece of music without first playing at least a few scales to loosen and supple his fingers. The horse is no exception to this universal problem.

At the beginning of a young horse's training, these daily 'preliminaries' will in effect comprise his entire daily routine, and with maximum priority and stress given to the first two. Eventually, perhaps after six months and when the horse is becoming nicely established in his ability and strength to work under a rider, the loosening phase will be reduced to five minutes, the stretching to a similar length of time, and the suppling to perhaps ten or fifteen, the whole preparatory process being completed and the horse ready for concentrated work in about twenty minutes or thereabouts.

LOOSENING

It can with some truth be said that the loosening process is never-ending and continues not only throughout the three preliminary phases but indeed throughout the entire training programme. But in the context in which we are considering it, it involves the removal, by calm and undemanding movement, of the main muscular lesions and contractions resulting from prolonged periods of inactivity in the stable.

This process should consist of nothing more than walking on a loose rein for about five minutes, including walking over a few poles on the ground or three or four very low cavaletti . . . all on a loose rein. The walk should be lively but in no way hurried, the object being to let the horse get some fresh-air in his lungs, his circulation going, and to flex his joints. He will also have a look at his surroundings and take note of any strange objects or other horses working in the same area.

At the end of this period, and particularly if it has become a part of the regular daily routine, the horse should be calm in his mind and loose in his body and limbs.

STRETCHING

With the horse now loose and attentive, we can begin the second phase of the preparatory exercises in which we try to stretch the main locomotory muscles, so that subsequently they can be suppled. A horse can often be seen doing a certain amount of stretching for himself as, for example, when he gets up from lying down and deliberately stretches at least one of his hindlegs. He will deal in that way, and up to a point, with anything that is obviously and uncomfortably stiff, but we want to deal in a thoroughly efficient manner with all the muscles that we know he is going to have to use in the next half-hour or so.

We cannot usefully tell the horse to stretch anything, nor can we force him to. He does not understand words; he does not understand the object of the exercise; and he would react to any degree of force with resistance and muscle contraction. We can therefore only do this work by arranging things so that he moves in a manner that will automatically stretch at least some of the muscles. Only the horse can do the stretching, but he must do it without conscious thought.

We cannot stretch the horse's spine, or any other bone. We are only concerned with stretching his muscles, and the easiest ones to deal with first are the big and long ones that exist and operate from the haunches through the back to the shoulders, neck, poll and jaw. They are also by far the most important as they have an overriding control over virtually everything the horse does. They also have to support the rider.

We cannot make the horse literally pull those muscles out from rear to front, to make them longer, any more than we could do a similar thing with our own back muscles no matter whether we are sitting down or standing up. But we can stretch the outer perimeter of a crooked stick that we want to straighten, just by bending both ends downwards with the fingers, around the fulcrum of the two thumbs pressing upwards on the underside. Done quietly for a few moments, and with some intermittent increasing and decreasing of the downward pressure of the fingers to create a little heat in the area of the fulcrum, the originally contracted side of the stick will become longer and better matched with the opposite side. The stick will become straight. We have stretched the wood and the bark on one side.

We can use exactly the same method to stretch those all-important muscles that run along the top line of the horse. Ultimately we need them to be both strong and supple, but before they can be developed in either of those ways they must be stretched.

With the stick, we passed both the ends downwards, stretching them over the retained fulcrum of the thumbs. With the horse, we also want to lower both ends, the head-and-neck and the haunches, so that the back muscles will be drawn tautly, and stretched, over the fulcrum of the withers.

The withers, being the vertical processes of the vertebrae that lie

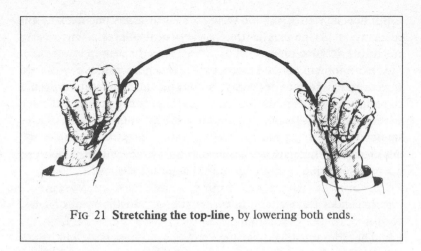

FIG 21 **Stretching the top-line**, by lowering both ends.

between the shoulder-blades, are not fixed at a specific height from the ground by any direct joint with the forelimbs, as are the vertebrae of the croup with the hindlegs. The withers, slung as it were from the shoulders by very powerful muscles and ligaments, together with the rest of the ribcage and thorax, are susceptible to only very slightly upward or downward height variation which can in practice be ignored for the purpose of this exercise. They retain their position quite firmly enough to provide the fulcrum around which we want to stretch the back-muscles.

The rear-end of the horse can only be lowered a little, and then only by inducing the horse to flex and keep flexed the three main joints of his hindlegs, thus reducing the overall length of those two limbs that support the croup. This is not easy to do, particularly with a young horse, and would in any case produce insufficient results on its own.

For the time being therefore, we shall be much better advised to concentrate on the very much easier and more productive problem of the front end, or the neck and poll. Fortunately the horse has no difficulty whatever in lowering his neck whenever he wishes or is willing to cooperate with the wishes of his rider. But we shall want him to position and retain it for relatively short periods considerably lower than he would normally carry it when in motion, although at slow paces he can easily carry it much lower as when grazing. There is consequently no need for anxiety that we might be imposing any excessive or uncomfortable strain on the horse.

106

But how do we set about lowering the horse's head and neck to the point when his nose is at least as low as the level of his chest; preferably down to the level of his knees; or perhaps even lower still? This is a problem about which the inexperienced rider should seek advice, and even watch a demonstration, before trying it for himself. In reality it is not too difficult for any reasonably good rider who understands the aids and has acquired a degree of feel for what is happening under the saddle. There are certain specific aids, as we shall see, and there are certain definite principles within which the rider must work and apply his aids. The principles are:

a The rider cannot, and must not try to, pull the head or neck down.

b The rider must 'get' his horse to lower his own neck and head.

c Once the head is down to an acceptable level, it must not be held or retained there by force through the reins, notwithstanding that it will be the rider's purpose to retain the low position for at least one full twenty-metre circle or the equivalent.

d The low-stretching exercise can be done at the walk or the trot, and even, though less frequently, at the canter. It may be easier to begin the lesson at the walk, though it is from the trot that the greatest benefit will accrue by reason of the greater swing of the back-muscles in that gait through the moment of suspension when all the limbs are free. In that moment, as with a swimmer who is suspended in the water, the whole body is free of contraction. But that free swinging of the back in trot will be of particular importance when we come to consider the final phase of these preparatory exercises, that of strengthening after suppling.

e For the exercise to be effective in exerting a genuine stretching effect, the horse must be retained 'on the bit', with all that that implies, throughout the lowering, and to whatever degree of lowering is achieved. Any sceptic who doubts the importance of being on the bit for the efficient working of a horse's back can test the matter for himself. Let him stand upright and then stretch down to touch his toes. In doing that he will need, unless he is exceptionally athletic, to keep his chin in, and point the top of his head towards the ground and his toes. He will, in that position, undoubtedly feel the pull on the back muscles as they are stretched over his curved spine.

But now, while still keeping his fingers on or near his toes, let him

107

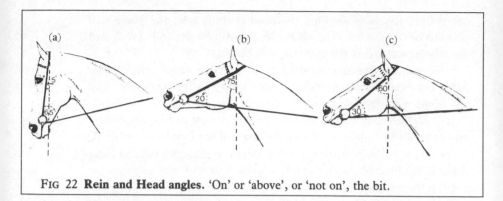

FIG 22 **Rein and Head angles.** 'On' or 'above', or 'not on', the bit.

tip back his neck, poke his chin forward, and look straight ahead parallel to the ground. He will immediately and assuredly feel the muscles of his back, from the shoulders downward, begin to hollow and contract. He has in effect done the equivalent of what the horse does with his head and neck when it comes 'above the bit', with precisely similar results to the back-muscles.

One of the many factors involved in a horse being 'on the bit' is that the reins should be making an open or broad angle with the horse's head, say between sixty and seventy degrees. If the angle of the rein and the head is reduced or closed by the poking forward of the nose, to perhaps fifty or forty degrees, the action of the bit will tend to slide up the jaw and so eventually back through the neck instead of direct to the rider's hand. In doing that it will nullify the essential lever action and forward flow of muscle action through the neck, poll and jaw. The poll will become rigid and eventually there will be blockage of the muscle-flow in the area of the withers.

It follows that, since the rein and head angle must remain approximately the same no matter at what height the horse may be carrying his head, so the angle of the gullet, between the neck and the head, will remain approximately the same whether the horse's head is high or low, if we want him to be on the bit.

That leads us to the crucial issue that we have to face concerning the angle of the head to the ground. If the horse remains 'on the bit' according to the criteria outlined in the previous two paragraphs, his head or face-line will inevitably come increasingly behind the vertical as his neck stretches forward and down below the horizontal. It cannot be otherwise, unless he comes, in effect, above the bit. If it is

108

not behind the vertical when the head is really low, the horse will cease to be 'on the bit'; the back-muscles will be flat and static; and the whole purpose of the exercise will be lost.

This aspect of the stretching exercise has been dealt with in some detail because it is often said, perhaps somewhat pedantically, that any horse with its head behind the vertical is, *ipso facto*, 'overbent'. Certainly, overbending is one of the cardinal sins of dressage training, but it cannot be judged solely by the angle of the face to the ground. The totality of the posture has to be assessed, that is to say the face-angle in conjunction with the gullet-angle and with the angle of the neck to the ground.

For example, the horse's neck will be very high when performing a levade or a courbette, in the latter case perhaps almost vertical. The face-line will on those occasions be at an angle with the ground of forty-five or, in the case of the courbette, nearly ninety degrees; angles which would be totally unacceptable in more normal activities. Yet no one will suggest that those horses are 'above the bit'.

It is surely clear that the angle or height of the neck is ultimately the deciding factor on where we expect the face-line to be when the horse is 'on the bit'. We should therefore put our faith in the logic of that argument and accept the consequent fact that we cannot efficiently stretch a horse's back muscles by lowering his head towards the ground unless at the same time he brings his nose somewhat behind the vertical. But the ultimate proof of that conviction will be found in the wonderful feel that we get from the swing in and through the back of our horse as we practise the exercise in the manner described. It will tell us all we could wish to know about the freedom and physical contentment of the horse and the beneficial effect on the length and cadence of his steps.

LOWERING THE QUARTERS

To a very large extent the lowering of the quarters, which we have already noted as being difficult to achieve as the direct result of action by the rider, will happen almost automatically as the direct consequence of stretching the back muscles through the neck. The increased forward and upward swing and lift of the back muscles will have the effect of slightly arching the back, and that will facilitate the ability of the horse to bend or flex downwards the rear end of his spine at the only point at which it is capable of such flexion, i.e., at the junction of the lumbar vertebrae and the sacroiliac joint. It can only be a comparatively slight flexion but it is sufficient to produce a repositioning of the pelvis that will enable the hindlegs to be engaged further forward under the horse than usual. Thus we begin to see, and to feel, the completed arc, or overall stretch, that we first spoke of in connection with the bent stick (Fig. 21), and of which we shall be speaking again in the last section of this chapter.

In the long run it is this overall and continuous arc, or arch, of muscle-tension from the mouth through the poll, neck, back, haunches and hindlegs to the hindfeet that gives us the combination of power and collection that makes everything seem possible with a well trained horse.

It is often said that a horse that is calm and relaxed will of his own accord take the reins through the rider's fingers and stretch his own head and neck down towards the ground if he is allowed and encouraged to do so by a gentle release of the rein-contact. But in practice the stretching does not occur quite so easily or so often. Maybe our horse is not so relaxed as we thought it was; or maybe its back is a little stiff, because we have not trained it as well as we hoped we had, and so the horse finds it difficult or uncomfortable to stretch the not-too-supple muscles and prefers to continue to go along in the more or less horizontal posture that he is used to. But whatever the reason, most riders will more frequently than not be faced with the situation in which the hoped-for downward stretch does not materialise. The horse needs help. He has to be shown how, and then encouraged by direct aids, to stretch in the manner, and to the degree that we wish; and to do so on demand. We cannot afford the time in our daily session to wait twenty minutes for him to consent. And we shall invariably find that the horse, once he has understood what we want and has by a little practise got over the problem of hitherto stiff muscles, will invariably enjoy this work, although we shall not continue it for very long at a time, in the same way that we do not necessarily prolong our own bedroom-floor exercises. A little is enough, provided it is done regularly most days.

It should be said here that stretching exercises should certainly have been included in the lunge-programme that, it is hoped, preceded the backing of the horse. If it was, that will have greatly

FIG 23 **Riding 'long and low'**, to stretch the muscles of the back and top-line; to enable the horse to lower his quarters and consequently to engage his hindlegs towards centre of gravity; and so to retain and develop balance and improve the elasticity of the paces. The horse does not come onto his forehand, despite the low head.

assisted the subsequent work under the saddle, because the horse's back will have been in good order from the start.

Stretching exercises on the lunge are somewhat easier for the horse than when done mounted, because there is then no weight on his back to depress and inhibit its swing. But it is a rather more subtle matter for the trainer, and it is proposed here to deal only with the aids for the mounted version of the work. But remember only that all work done on the lunge is fun; that the horse enjoys it and finds it easy; and that lessons first taught on the lunge pay very big dividends when it comes to repeating them later from the saddle. The trainer also can learn a very great deal from the lunge.

111

THE AIDS FOR STRETCHING

The first thing that we have to do is to work on or overcome the stiffness, amounting to resistance, that we know must exist to a greater or lesser extent if the horse will not easily reach forward and down to find the bit when we invite him to by a gentle release of the contact combined with continuing forward drive from the legs. That stiffness will be immediately apparent in the neck and the poll and that, fortunately, is the area in which it is most easy to break down any stiffness because we have the reins to help us. We break down muscular stiffness by flexing the muscles in question, and in the case of muscles in the neck it is easier to flex or bend them laterally rather than longitudinally. So our plan will be to bend the neck and poll laterally, by direct use of the reins and then, when the horse begins to feel more supple in that area, to ask him to bend and stretch himself longitudinally. It is in the latter direction that the reins are of little use to us.

We will begin with the side we feel the horse is most able and willing to bend, say to the left. The manner in which we go about it is as follows, working at the rising trot and a large circle to the left.

a We keep a firm and steady contact on the right or 'outside' rein, taking particular care to keep the right hand still so that it will not make any demands on the horse.

b We take a gentle, short, slow 'take' with the left rein, mainly by lifting the hand a little while turning the little finger to the inside and closing all the fingers on the rein. In doing this we should be careful not to move our left elbow to the rear as this would result in a direct and forceful pull on the horse's mouth, which is always wrong in any circumstances. We should be able to obtain the left flexion that we want by means of the hand, wrist, fingers and forearm only.

c We have asked for the flexion, but we do not continue to ask for it by fixing the hand. As soon as the horse 'gives' to our request by bending a little to the left, we immediately return the compliment and say 'thank you' by giving the rein back to him, even to the extent of momentarily releasing all contact on that side. But we still keep the contact unaltered on the outside as we want the horse to keep working into that rein. And for that latter purpose we must also remember to use our inside leg well forward on the girth to keep the horse going forward and at the same time to encourage him to bend round it as he flexes in the neck.

d We repeat the combined inside-leg-and-rein aid, always with its complementary release, and we continue repeating it until the horse becomes consistently light on the left side of the neck and mouth. This may take us anything from two or three to seven or eight demands.

e When we feel it to be opportune, and as we release a request from the left hand, we give a little with the right rein, as an invitation to the horse to lengthen his neck while still keeping that right contact. If we get no lengthening response the first time, we shall surely be lucky at the second or third try and as the horse begins to appreciate what is being offered to him. But as soon as he does give that first and probably tentative response, the rider should quickly pat him firmly and twice on the neck with his right hand, even though that means releasing the rein contact for a second or two. The rein need not be dropped, or transferred to the other hand, the pat being quite adequately made with the fingers of the closed fist still holding the rein. Horses are very quick to understand and respond to the simple pat on the neck, and will invariably do what is being asked of them with greater confidence next time.

In this case the horse may very well be under the impression that it is somewhat improper for him to stretch his neck down towards the ground while trotting along. He may fear some sort of reprimand for doing so, as such action is at least a bit abnormal. So it is vital that he should be reassured that stretching is, curiously enough, just exactly what he is being asked to do. There is no better way of doing that than a pat on the neck. It will pay big dividends.

f It often happens that the horse, lacking confidence and faith in his first effort to stretch, will make a somewhat violent thrust of his head downwards in a manner that drags the rein out of the rider's hands, or pulls him out of the saddle. This of course is not the kind of response that we really want, and later on we should need to reprimand such action as it can do little good. But in these early stages, when we are tring to establish communication and confidence on the subject, it is wiser to tolerate the quick, relatively jerky action and even to congratulate the horse, treating his action as at least a sign of understanding and willingness to oblige. But after a while the rough action must be tactfully restrained and converted into a smooth 'taking down' of the bit and eventually a drawing of the reins through the riders fingers when the hand cannot reach far enough.

g When the horse first takes the outside rein down, the rider need not worry if he loses the softness on the inside. Be satisfied with one thing at a time. But once confidence in the stretching procedure is established, the rider must try to retain the inside softness during the downward stretch, and also to retain it while the horse moves forward for several strides in the stretched posture. He does this by lightly and gently continuing the same inside leg-and-hand demand as often as he thinks necessary to discourage or pre-empt the horse's fairly natural inclination to take hold of the inside rein again, to match the contact on the outside. If he does that, he will become stiff again, losing his ability to move forward in the low and stretched posture. Very light and sensitive hands are needed at this stage to enable the rider to maintain the rein-control but at the same time to do nothing that might inhibit the horse from relaxing and stretching. A slightly excessive action by either hand or change of balance can easily cause the horse to raise his neck and head, in which event the whole process must be restarted.

h We continue to work in this way on the left rein and on the large circle until we can with some confidence obtain at least a modest measure of success; that is to say until we can lower the head and neck on demand so that the horse's neck will be a little below the horizontal and his nose at least to the level of his chest. In the longer run we shall not be satisfied until we can at any time put his neck and head down so that his nose is about the level of his knees or even, ultimately, within a few inches of the ground, should we so desire it. Then, and perhaps only then, will we know for certain that our horse is totally relaxed and stretched, and not holding something back.

i When we are confident of the first stage to chest-level on the left rein, we can begin the same task on the opposite or right rein and circle, and later work both sides alternatively or as the circumstances and progress of the horse seems to indicate.

j The rider's ability to stretch and lower his horse in this manner and at any time may be used as a valuable test of any horse's suppleness and obedience to the aids, and indeed of the rider's knowledge of and ability to coordinate the aids. That test is valid and relevant to all stages of training, from the lunge through novice, medium, advanced and grand-prix levels. It should never be

114

neglected or taken for granted because the more advanced the training becomes, the greater the stress that is imposed on the horse's back and the greater the inevitable tendency for the back muscles to become contracted and stiff. The greater the need, therefore, for the preventative or remedial stretching exercises.

k The stretching work should ideally be done daily and just for a few moments, say for a couple of circles at the trot on each rein, provided that the response is found to be correct and satisfactory or until it becomes so, immediately after the preliminary walk on a loose rein and before any work 'on the bit' is started. Only then can we be sure that the horse is physically ready for work 'on the bit' and only then will it be wise or fair to make maximum demands on the horse. A few moments of stretching can also and usefully be introduced at some point during the course of the work session, should the horse seem to be getting tired or a little stiff, and just for general mental as well as physical relaxation. There is no doubt whatever that stretching is a supreme exercise for relaxing the horse's mind. A mentally tense horse always stiffens his back, but once the back is relaxed he will begin to listen to his rider and to work with enjoyment.

l Throughout the work, the horse must be ridden down by the use of forward-driving legs and coordinating rein-aids. It is useless, and the exercise will probably fail altogether, if the rider does nothing with his legs and merely lets the rein go loose, hoping that the horse will choose to lower himself and continue at a steady pace and rhythm. In those circumstances, should there by chance be some lowering, the horse will not be 'on the bit'; it will probably poke its nose; and the back will remain flat because the muscles cannot be worked unless the horse is 'on the bit'. The rider himself must do the job purposefully and deliberately, as an act of horsemanship, retaining full control of his horse throughout the process and for as long as he wishes. There is an old and valid horseman's proverb that says 'Nothing that the horse does entirely of his own accord is of any value'.

m Once the horse has understood and will accept the aids to stretch low-and-long, but remaining steady on the bit and therefore somewhat behind the vertical with his head, he should be ridden actively forward and into the hand by judicious seat and leg aids to develop and strengthen the muscular pulsations through the back and neck; to encourage the haunches to lower and the hindlegs to engage further forward under the centre of gravity where they will take additional weight off the forehand despite the lowness of the neck; and to increase the length and swing of the stride. When this stage is reached the horse will begin to give himself to the rider who will experience a noticeable swing and cadence under the saddle such as he will seldom have when working his horse, however well trained he may be, in the more normal posture.

This is however, strong work, and it should not be used to excess or to the point when the horse may begin to think that he is expected only and always to work in that manner. But nonetheless, a little and fairly often can do nothing but good and will assuredly give pleasure to both parties.

n We can end this description on the longitudinal stretching exercise with a few additional but important tips. (1) The horse must not be allowed to hurry his rhythm or go too fast, because that would make it too difficult to keep his balance in the low posture and he will begin to be afraid of going down. A quiet and very steady pace is essential, at least until confidence is fully established. (2) The rider must never think of trying to hold the horse's head down or at any particular angle by the reins. The neck and head posture must be totally natural and will come of its own accord provided only that the horse is ridden forward into the bit with the normal contact and with the aids already described. To retain that posture for a more or less prolonged period, it is only necessary to continue with the same sequence and coordination of aids. (3) It is most profitably practised at the trot because the moment of suspension between each stride permits the maximum swing through the back to develop the muscles.

A WARNING

Finally, a word of warning to the inexperienced rider. There are sceptics, and those of little faith, who will be heard saying that this stretching, or low-and-long, exercise is a dangerous thing because (they say) it tends to put the horse onto its forehand, and this may happen to an extent that the horse may never be reclaimed or brought back into collection. That argument may be listened to, thought about, and then retained in the back of the mind. But it is not valid for

FIG 24 **Not on the bit with high neck** (see Fig. 22 and 23); flat back; and hindlegs not engaged towards C of G. Horse has excess weight on the forehand and is unable to shift it back, despite high head carriage. The stiffness and flatness of the back prevents the lengthening or elasticity of the paces.

a reasonably competent rider, and none other should be training a dressage horse.

Certainly the exercise should not be used to excess, as has already been acknowledged, but that qualification applies to most of the good things in life. We should not eat, drink or even sing to excess, for fear of retribution of some kind. We should not warm our cold hands too closely at the fire, for fear of burning them. But knowing the danger, we all take that risk for the ultimate benefit of our health.

A horse can be 'on its forehand' even when its head is high in the air because then the back muscles are restricted and the quarters consequently unable to lower and engage to lighten the forehand.

Left to himself, in a relatively inactive state, the horse is naturally weighted on his forehand. He can only relieve that weight by lowering and engaging his quarters and hindlegs, and he can only do that when the back is free and swinging.

FIG 25 BRONCO BUSTER by Frederic Remington. The ability of a horse to lower his quarters and utilise the muscles of his back when he really means business.

There is no easier or more effective way of freeing and making the back muscles swing than lowering and stretching the neck over the fulcrum of the withers. Then the horse is in the best possible position to engage his hindlegs to take the weight off his forehand and, in the process, to so strengthen his loin muscles that he will be the better able to keep his forehand light even when he is ridden in the normal posture.

Finally, look at the picture of the buck-jumper (Fig. 25) and notice how the lowered neck and well rounded back enable the horse to lower his quarters from the croup and engage his hindlegs. There can be few better examples of the tremendous power available to a horse that can round and use his back.

When the rider has learnt how to call on and make use of that power for his own purposes, he can claim to be a horseman.

The Whip and the Spurs

THE WHIP AND THE spur form auxilliary aids which should be used with great discretion and never casually or unintentionally. They should never be used in anger. The rider must learn to position his hands (for the whip) and his legs (for the spur) so that he can confidently comply with those principles.

The main purposes of the whip and the spur are to support the leg-aid and to enliven any sluggish response to the latter by the horse. Aids of the spur should never be used as punishment which, if necessary, should always be given by strictly controlled application of the whip close behind the rider's leg.

THE WHIP AID

The whip should be carried at its point of balance in either hand in such a manner that its presence does not cause any alteration to the normal position of the hand which naturally is also holding the rein or reins. With the hand held in that perfectly normal and correct position, the whip will be found to lie lightly against the side of the thigh and more or less parallel to the rider's lower leg. To use the whip as an auxilliary aid as already outlined, the rider slightly raises the tail of the whip by an inward twist of the hand, but without altering the general position of the hand relative to the horse's mouth or his own elbow. Then, with a more or less sharp reverse or outward twist of the wrist, the middle or thick part of the whip falls against the rider's thigh, causing the thin end to flick sharply against the horse, just behind the rider's boot.

The whip should never be used except in conjunction with and in support of a leg-aid. It should be used immediately after the leg-aid, and only if the leg-aid has not been successful or has been ignored. In the latter case the whip will follow as a reminder or light reprimand. Horses do not like the touch of the whip, though they are seldom afraid of it, and so they will learn to avoid its use by responding more promptly or actively to the initial aid from the leg. So the reaction to the normal aids is improved and the rider/horse relationship becomes ever more subtle.

For all normal schooling purposes, the tap of the whip across the rider's thigh is entirely sufficient. Only in cases of extreme disobedience justifying severe punishment should the whip-hand be removed from the reins to give the full stroke with the whip.

The whip is an essential part of every rider's equipment, though it should be used somewhat infrequently, usually gently, and always with a clear-cut intention or purpose. It should always complement or assist a seat or leg-aid, but should never be used as a substitute for either.

All horses have a natural respect for the whip, but they should also be trained from an early stage to understand but not to fear it. It should be long enough to touch the horse's flank without displacing the hand, but not so long that there will be a risk of it touching the horse unexpectedly.

A horseman without a whip is at a severe disadvantage.

THE SPUR AID

The spur is by no means essential for the efficient schooling of a young horse, and indeed it is better not to use it at all in the early stages because of the danger of a ticklish horse acquiring the habit of kicking against it.

The spur is used to give point, when necessary, to the aids which are applied by the rider's leg through the large area of soft, leather boot. In the long run the spur will become almost redundant with a well schooled horse as the accomplished rider transfers more and more of his aids from his legs to his seat and loin.

Blunt spurs are preferred to those with any form of rowel, except for some exceptionally dull, lazy or obstinate horses. Sharp rowels are merely cruel.

The correct use of the spur is to draw the end forwards and into touch with the horse by turning the toe out and the heel in. This method ensures that the spur operates on the same principle as the normal use of the lower leg that has already been described, but it will not disturb the seat or the length of the leg. Both leg and spur act to increase forward activity by pressing inwards and forwards against the horse in a logical manner. The spur should never be used so that the end prods backwards into the horse's flanks so as to bruise them.

The old-fashioned method of kicking backwards with the leg or with the spur in order to make the horse go forwards has nothing to commend it. There is no logic in it and it can only cause confusion. If the spur is used, it will also cause pain or worse.

The horse soon becomes aware of the spur as a constant threat, but it should seldom be put to the test. A very gentle touch is sufficient at all times.